"Biomimicry and Business is exa t now – examples of people successully practicing biomimicry to help heal their part of the world. This book represents the next step and will be important in the annals of this emerging discipline."
— *Janine Benyus, author of* Biomimicry: Innovation Inspired by Nature *and cofounder of Biomimicry 3.8 and the Biomimicry Institute.*

"Normally, people refer to four types of ecosystem services: provisioning, regulating, cultural and supporting. Farnsworth reminds us of an often-overlooked fifth service: mentoring. Mother Nature can be a coach on product design, business model design, the circular economy, operational efficiencies and strategic planning. Smart businesses learn from Mother Nature. This books shows how we all can."
— *Bob Willard, Chief Sustainability Champion, Sustainability Advantage.*

"Margo Farnsworth's *Biomimicry and Business* elegantly shows how innovative firms are embracing a new business approach to solve complex design challenges. This book provides a great introduction to the world of biomimicry through the lens of business and entrepreneurship and gives readers practical tools and resources for integrating the biomimicry methodology in their corporate organizations. The author's detailed business case studies provide more color on how the biomimicry process is used and implemented successfully across of variety of companies. There are many lessons to be discovered here and I believe that everyone interested in regenerative design should read this book."
— *Jacques Chirazi, Director of Student Entrepreneurship and Blackstone LaunchPad, University of California, San Diego, and Managing Partner + Founder, Biomimicry, Switzerland.*

"The book contains a nice mix of conceptual spadework and real stories, with the "bonus" of straightforward yet gentle guidance from the author in taking up the challenges of risk and change. It will be a source of inspiration."
— *Gavin Van Horn, Creative Director and Executive Editor, Center for Humans and Nature.*

"This is an important book. Our planet is in crisis, and a great deal of environmentalist discourse has been pointing out that we may have to choose between capitalism and the planet. No matter its truth, this rhetoric can be paralyzing. Focused on the enormous picture and on what we need to stop doing, it can make action seem pointless or just too difficult and painful. People turn off and put their heads back in the sand or, even worse, decide they better squeeze out what's left from the planet while they can because we're all doomed anyway. *Biomimicry and Business* imagines another way forward. Using an appealingly positive and pragmatic approach, Farnsworth demonstrates that business can do good by being good. By learning and utilizing the principles of biomimicry, entrepreneurs can be kinder to the environment and more innovative and profitable. Yet, Farnsworth doesn't just make this claim, she shows her readers how to do it – with jargon-free prose, entertaining case studies (from her own interviews), and concise and clear guidelines."

– Sara Crosby, Associate Professor of English,
The Ohio State University at Marion.

BIOMIMICRY AND BUSINESS

Biomimicry, the practice of observing then mimicking nature's strategies to solve business challenges, offers a path to healthy profit while working in partnership, and even reciprocity, with the natural world. Other books have described biomimicry, its uses, and its benefits. This book shows readers how to create their own biomimetic or bioinspired solutions with clear benefits to the bottom line, the environment, and people.

Fashioned through storytelling, this book blends snapshots of five successful companies – Nike, Interface, Inc., PAX Scientific, Sharklet Technologies, and Encycle – which decided to partner with nature by deploying biomimicry, The book details how they discovered the practices, introduced them to staff, engaged in the process, and measured outcomes. The book concludes with challenges for readers to determine their own next steps in business and offers practical and useful resources to get there.

By revealing the stories of each professional's journey with lessons they learned, then providing resources and issuing a challenge and pathway to do business better, this book serves as a tool for entrepreneurs, seasoned professionals, and students to emulate nature's brilliance, apply it at work, and contribute to a healthier, more prosperous world.

Margo Farnsworth is a writer and biomimicry educator. She has served as faculty and visiting faculty, and advises students internationally as a Fellow for the Biomimicry Institute. Farnsworth has also worked as a naturalist, Executive Director, and Senior Fellow for a Southeastern watershed organization advising two Federal administrations.

BIOMIMICRY AND BUSINESS

HOW COMPANIES ARE USING NATURE'S STRATEGIES TO SUCCEED

Margo Farnsworth

LONDON AND NEW YORK

First published 2021
by Routledge
2 Park Square, Milton Park, Abingdon, Oxon OX14 4RN

and by Routledge
52 Vanderbilt Avenue, New York, NY 10017

Routledge is an imprint of the Taylor & Francis Group, an informa business

© 2021 Margo Farnsworth

The right of Margo Farnsworth to be identified as author of this work has been asserted by her in accordance with sections 77 and 78 of the Copyright, Designs and Patents Act 1988.

All rights reserved. No part of this book may be reprinted or reproduced or utilised in any form or by any electronic, mechanical, or other means, now known or hereafter invented, including photocopying and recording, or in any information storage or retrieval system, without permission in writing from the publishers.

Trademark notice: Product or corporate names may be trademarks or registered trademarks, and are used only for identification and explanation without intent to infringe.

British Library Cataloguing-in-Publication Data
A catalogue record for this book is available from the British Library

Library of Congress Cataloging-in-Publication Data
Names: Farnsworth, Margo, 1959– author.
Title: Biomimicry and business: how companies are using nature's strategies to succeed / Margo Farnsworth.
Description: Milton Park, Abingdon, Oxon; New York, NY: Routledge, 2021. | Includes bibliographical references and index.
Identifiers: LCCN 2020020474 (print) | LCCN 2020020475 (ebook) | ISBN 9780367549206 (hardback) | ISBN 9780367552596 (paperback) | ISBN 9781003092605 (ebook)
Subjects: LCSH: Business planning. | Biomimicry—Case studies.
Classification: LCC HD30.28 .F36 2021 (print) | LCC HD30.28 (ebook) | DDC 658.4/012—dc23
LC record available at https://lccn.loc.gov/2020020474
LC ebook record available at https://lccn.loc.gov/2020020475

ISBN: 978-0-367-54920-6 (hbk)
ISBN: 978-0-367-55259-6 (pbk)
ISBN: 978-1-003-09260-5 (ebk)

Typeset in Bembo Std
by codeMantra

CONTENTS

	Preface	viii
1	Making a Living	1
2	On Mountain Goats and Citizenship – The Nike Story of Biomimicry	11
3	What is Biomimicry and Why Use It?	23
4	Business from the Wild – Interface, Inc.	36
5	Spiraling Into Success – PAX Scientific	51
6	Nurse Sharks in Your Hospital – Sharklet Technologies, Inc.	62
7	The Blackout and the Bee – Encycle	74
8	So What?	86
9	Now What?	97
10	One More Thing	113
	Afterword	127
	Index	131

PREFACE

ABSTRACT

Discerning harm from the many ways we do business doesn't require extensive research – only a plane ride across the country. Looking down, a passenger can see waste flowing from murky rivers through cities and agriculture runoff from our rural areas, ill-conceived harvesting of forest lumber and minerals as one views land stripped bare, and clues to increasing scarcities of resources like water in regions where perfect circles reveal moisture where it doesn't normally appear. The author narrates these in a coast-to-coast display. There is an alternative to the continued standard rev of our industrial horsepower though – a way some businesses are taking steps to do better.

Readers will learn the stories of men and women deploying biomimicry and its relatives in business today. They're sometimes tales of overcoming adversity or capitalizing on a lightbulb moment. Here, the author lays out the challenges and invites us to explore how we can create success in business with less harm to both people and planet. Readers learn they will explore companies engaging in biomimicry and its affiliates which benefit their economic bottom lines while also delivering them happier clients, healthier colleagues, and the beginnings of recovery for the planet.

> Tell me a fact and I'll learn. Tell me a truth and I'll believe.
> But tell me a story and it will live in my heart forever.
> – Indian Proverb

PREFACE **ix**

THE POWER OF STORY IN BUSINESS

This book began with an early afternoon liftoff that brought my gaze from the heat mirage of the tarmac out to the Pacific Ocean and the sweep of the horizon beyond. I always expect to see a whale on these flights. I never do, but I always expect it. As we turned toward the far edge of the continent, I began my cross-country game. First, I knew, came the rich agricultural fields of the West Coast. The blooms of algae gave away the secrets of what run off fields into the rivers creating a soup of fertilizer, herbicides, pesticides, and topsoil which aggregate a portion of the *real* cost of food. As we flew east, the polka dots of irrigation signaled water used where none is naturally present above ground. I drank my coffee as scars of mines and clear-cutting appeared across the Rockies, Midwest, and Appalachia. It was cold and dark as the plane descended over the Potomac River dumping its urban runoff into the Chesapeake Bay and on into the Atlantic Ocean. I saw it all; and I thought about the story arc of the industrialized world. I thought about sharing biomimicry stories and how this book might help you, and it felt right.

Certainly, our beginnings in business were primitive and focused first on conquering nature, later expanding production of the widgets and gadgets we felt improved our lives. During our country's first steps, we wanted and needed to overcome the inconveniences and sometimes dangers of muddy tracks with their seemingly bottomless potholes while traveling through dark woods between villages and towns. We sought ways to feed ourselves in a routine and safe manner. Accomplishing daily needs required most of our waking hours. Comfort, money, and the promise of upward mobility for the businessmen delivering an increasing number of inventions to individuals, who probably even then sought to keep up with the Jones's, enticed us into easier and evermore convenient lives. The lure of invention – swivel chairs and coffee percolators, air conditioners, blenders, and eventually computers – made our eyes sparkle.

As the centuries turned, we began noticing changes in our once clear skies, forest views, and crystalline lakes. Some days, yellowish was the sky color children saw when they peered out of their classrooms across many cities. Although advances have been made in air quality, we often see the same color and air quality warnings now routinely appear on sultry, summer days. In our forests, millions of acres have been clear-cut. Today many professionals practice the more conservation-oriented selective cutting. Still, an area larger than 3,000,000 football fields is clear cut every year in the U.S. alone, leaving bare slopes to erode[1] and habitat lost. And on the west coast, tens of thousands of river miles and hundreds of thousands of acres of lakes, bays, and wetlands are now either not swimmable or fishable – sometimes neither.[2] Volatile organic compounds and hospital-acquired infections tax our health. Increasing needs for energy, waste reduction, water, and its treatment all converge around our natural resources.

As all of this has blossomed, some in business began seeking kinder ways to do their work here and there, taking into account the state of Earth and the people they employed in addition to profit. Some didn't. Regulations were developed and followed – or not. Earth had begun revealing consequences from the exertion of pressure placed on its many resources. Natural systems were straining even as those few businesses and progressive governments began evolving to heal what had been abused through ignorance, neglect, or prioritization of the bottom line over all else. The time came when we acknowledged we must modify the way we do business. We had been failing Earth and, much to our surprise, it was beginning to falter.

Fortunately, more business leaders have begun to notice the changes and started to question the long view. People who cared, asked for, and demanded more sustainable practices – and began backing up those demands with their purse strings. Slowly, the industrial wheels began to change course further. Energy-saving practices and water conservation appeared in some offices, warehouses, and other facilities. Corporate sustainability reports dotted the Dow Jones landscape, but many have realized this could only be the beginning in our shift to benign and even restorative practices. Much more is required to relieve a straining planet.

$$\approx$$

So, why should we read stories to address these sometimes overwhelming problems alongside the challenges we face in our businesses? One good reason is because we want to experience success, and the most successful businesses and other enterprises often start

PREFACE **xi**

with stories. They're sometimes tales of overcoming adversity or capitalizing on a lightbulb moment. There may be a rise to glory or a fall from grace. Either way, stories capture our attention. Telling stories of inspiration and illustrating pathways to success can move people toward action more than case studies and technical reports alone – although they too can help create change. While all of them are important, the best stories are written specifically in the language of the reader's everyday life instead of being fettered with an overage of jargon. Stories ignite our desires to know what happens next – especially when told in everyday language. They assist us in remembering what we read and help us integrate it into our work and world whether we are Chief Executive Officers, line workers on the factory floor, designers, or marketers of our products and services. Stories create equal access to ideas.

The following tales of biomimicry and its relatives arise from existing companies in vastly different fields from sportswear to carpeting, biomedical equipment, water treatment, and energy management companies. They were chosen because of the range of requirements and circumstances present in each and the varied paths of adoption and success each company experienced with biomimicry or related practices. Their innovation arcs were strewn with a blend of concerns for people – whether clients or employees, the planet, and of course, profit. Their solutions have either been inspired by nature or mimicked actual structures and processes found in nature. As you get to know the people in each company, you'll see how they integrated biomimicry and its relatives into their solution-making, then how they have advanced the methodologies into their companies to varying degrees. The stories and this book are meant for the tire kicker – the business person or student who may have heard of biomimicry but wants to know more before investing time on diving deep.

Today, business leaders are searching new vistas – those of working with nature instead of working to overcome it. If you are one of these, one of the people curious as to how to do well in business while in partnership with the planet, this book is for you. If you're not sure where to begin, this book is for you. If you're not sure how to overcome company inertia, this book is for you. You'll read first a little about how we got here and how we can create a form of reciprocity between nature and business to our mutual benefit.

You'll discover the pathways of a new brand of industrialist and entrepreneur – those who are doing well by doing good through consulting nature for answers to challenges their businesses encounter. You'll learn what biomimicry is to be sure and how these business leaders deployed and profited by it in their companies as well as how they are helping employees, clients, and the natural world outside their doors. In these pages, business professionals and entrepreneurs will find science in a palatable format. Engineers, designers, and biologists will discover business lessons learned without jargon and endless profit and loss tables. But the things that capture our imagination are the tales of adventure, of overcoming the odds and vanquishing the Goliath while doing business better for all. The power of their stories can spark the imagination, kindle a dream, offer tools and entrances to build businesses, help our human neighbors, and tend our planet's aching wounds. That's the book you hold in your hands. Later you can read the research papers and the technical briefs. You can access the business plans and the P&L statements – and you should. But for now, just enjoy the stories.

REFERENCES

1 United States Department of Agriculture. "U.S. Forest Resource Facts and Historical Trends." https://www.fia.fs.fed.us/library/brochures/docs/2012/ForestFacts_1952-2012_English.pdf. Accessed 29 August, 2014.

2 Cheng, Isaac and Thesing, Alicia. "California Regulation of Agricultural Runoff." *Environment, Energy, and Resources Section.* American Bar Association. https://www.americanbar.org/groups/environment_energy_resources/publications/trends/2017-2018/november-december-2017/california_regulation_of_agricultural_runoff/. Accessed 30 November, 2017.

MAKING A LIVING

Natura nihil fit in frustra.
Nature does nothing in vain.

It used to be just go to work. Make a living.

Most of us aren't raised with any notion of doing more than this in business. I certainly wasn't.

I was taught to think of my career as the vehicle to support myself and my family. The courses I took steeped me in knowledge handed down over time from businessmen and women, scientists and educators who had successfully laid the technological and business groundwork for companies, researchers and future public servants. Few of those courses included problem-solving strategies used by other organisms with whom we share the land, sea, and skies. Never were we taught to ask how they would accomplish a task.

While many of us may have a place in our hearts for or even take action on behalf of those organisms (the birds and the bees, the flowers and the trees), we seldom focus on them much in our professional lives. Information and guidance on Earth's other inhabitants regarding their health, populations, need for and availability of viable homes and food supplies, along with whatever strategies for success they may use, are cordoned off to our pre-career lives or later at least partially siloed away from paying work under titles like philanthropy or volunteerism. Even when corporate sustainability reports came into being, little if any professional training taught us anything about considering nature as a business partner and mentor. Who knew how profitable that partnership could be on so many levels across so many professions?

MAKING A LIVING

EXTENDING PARTNERSHIPS

Partnerships are commonplace in business. We generally think of them as relationships where some sort of exchange for mutual benefit takes place – a kind of reciprocity if you will. These exchanges, usually of ideas, goods, services, or finance, take place with other humans. This limited version of reciprocity and way of thinking is not our fault. It's how we were raised.

My father and his business partner dealt with exchanging goods and services for payment from customers. They sold pianos and each had his role in the company along with strategies for his accepted area of expertise. Dad eventually applied the same accepted business platform to several companies. He identified a consumer need or desire, usually spotted a partner with a complementary area of expertise and then responded to customer demands through product delivery. These customers subsequently paid for the product or service at a profit point acceptable to both parties. As the purchases became larger, the platform also included interest from financing as part of the equation. This was and is a common notion of business, so the customary reciprocity that lies within its forms of partnerships has become a standard format we recognize and follow.

This business model has been built on a foundation of financial and business resource metaphorical two-by-fours. If you examine the entire underpinning of the business though, you'll discover the real foundation of making a living ultimately resides in the presence, health, and abundance of our natural resources. Take the $200 billion annual forest product industry[1] for example. We regularly think of lumber being used for building and paper products. What we don't generally consider is the full scope of the products containing wood from crayons to coveralls and even more surprising products such as toothpaste and hairspray. Oh yes, and pianos. To make products like these, have the ability to sell them, or utilize raw materials for any of our work, raw materials must exist in the first place.

The abundance and quality of these living resources are reliant on physical forces such as temperature, precipitation, wind, and the seasons to which all living things must respond in some way or other. Living organisms, in turn, play parts in the cycles for water, nitrogen, and other necessary elements that move from air to Earth and back

MAKING A LIVING **3**

again – sustaining all life in the process. Often less clear but no less important are the relationships among these physical assets and cycles, and the plants, nonhuman animals, and other living beings which are also all part of our mutual support structure. We know Louisville Slugger is dependent on a plentiful supply of maple and ash trees for its popular bats. That kind of business we understand, complete with the transactions among lumber companies, the bat company and those businesses engaged in distribution. However, the business of those two particular trees also supports over 400 kinds of insects as well.[2]

This is one of the places where human enterprise has historically diverged from the broader requirements for reciprocity, life overall, and how planetary concerns have mixed and mingled with those of even a bat company. Let's take those 400 insect species and their roles. You probably remember from middle school science a little about the web of life, but unless you chose life sciences as a profession, the concepts may have been left back in the window seat of Mr. Smith's science classroom. No matter – here's why those lessons are critical to you now in business and in life. Of course, you know insects are a food source for ever larger animals up to and including animals we eat. However, their efforts in pollinating plants also deliver one out of every three bites of food we consume. As important, frankly more so to the folks at Louisville Slugger, in death they recycle nutrients that nourish those maple and ash trees allowing them to grow into the kind of trees our Major League Baseball players want to use for the big hits. Additionally, as those trees and other plants grow, they play a major role in, you guessed it, those cycles for water and nitrogen but also oxygen, carbon dioxide, phosphorous, and more – life stuff.

Within this big framework, life depends on those physical forces and a grand amalgam of organisms and their systems. We humans are part of those systems and also affect their abundance and quality as we make business and buying choices that directly influence them and their surroundings. Instead of simply harvesting raw materials from nature without much thought to all that supports them, leaders at more and more companies are beginning to build a new business model. They are beginning to recognize the value of our natural resources and their critical two-by-fours which support both our companies and our communities. These businesses are interfacing

4 MAKING A LIVING

directly with the world outside their doors by taking on nonhuman organisms as partners.

Our human partnerships have been based on relationships with colleagues who have generally been on Earth around the same amount of time as us (give or take a few years to a decade or so). Their well of knowledge, if different from ours, may go back a few hundred years to maybe a couple of thousand depending on the developmental expertise in their field of practice and experience they have amassed. But what if you could consult a business partner with a billion or so years of experience who had successfully adapted to become efficient with materials and energy? What if that partner could adapt to change easily? Would you be interested if they could integrate development with growth or be responsive to local conditions, which then helped you fine-tune your product or services?[3] Learning from these valuable skill sets could go a long way toward helping you make a living.

Such a partner exists right outside your door. The plants, animals, and other organisms there have been solving problems with structures, processes, and systems for longer than our own species has existed on Earth. While each person in a company doesn't actually need to understand every minute detail of nature in our day-to-day lives at the office, we do need to recognize and understand it provides those natural resource two-by-fours necessary for a firm business foundation. It can also offer problem-solving strategies which have successfully evolved over millennia whether you make bats, paint, or high-speed trains.

In the case of paint, the Sto Corporation mimicked the surface texture of lotus plants to reduce dirt's ability to adhere to painted surfaces. With StoColor® Lotusan® dirt simply runs off the painted plane when hit by rain or other liquids. This reduces both expense and impacts from potential toxicity of cleaning agents to organisms coming in contact with them or being affected by them as they run into storm drains and waterways. And all by observing how a lotus leaf sheds dirt. As a very different example of age-old expertise, consider how kingfishers and owls influenced the makers of high-speed trains. In Japan, the highly successful Shinkansen line connects thousands of people to major cities as they commute to work each day. Unfortunately, the company was challenged by complaints of noise pollution resulting from the pantographs (overhead wires used to electrically power the trains) and the sonic booms caused by air compression as trains exited tunnels on their routes. By emulating the silencing feather structure of owls for the overhead wires and the elegant streamlined beak shape of kingfishers (who dive into water for their dinners causing nary a wave), Japan Railway West was able to bring noise levels down, increase speed by 10%, and reduce energy required for operation by 15%, thereby using fewer natural resources in the process. Win, win, and win. We can observe, adapt, emulate, and deploy nature's strategies in new ways to do our work more efficiently and at less cost. We can create deeper partnerships and benefit numerous human and nonhuman communities through these partnerships by starting to ask, "How would a plant or bird solve this problem?" Indeed, what would an even broader examination of organisms and their strategies offer up to these questions?

Most of us are not instructed on the importance of or even possibilities present when we engage in partnership with Earth's other inhabitants. If we are not schooled on what it actually takes to create a firm foundation, choices we are presented with in business are unclear or incomplete. Often the fate of wildlife or plant communities seems far away and disconnected from our day-to-day lives. Seldom are we taught that they not only provide us with those necessary two-by-fours, but that we are so tied to them we will either all prosper or eventually fail together. However, if we look carefully, these consultants can reveal whole new course books of knowledge that yield competitive advantage for our businesses. If we make a few adjustments to our practices and technologies to better engage with and protect what lies beyond our doors, both for our sakes and for theirs, we can participate in a higher form of partnership moving into reciprocity, which can yield a firmer foundation for business and for all life on Earth.

THE ELEMENT OF RECIPROCITY

In the years leading up to this book, I championed the idea of protecting nature for economic benefits gained from ecosystem services. This is a far different kind of partnership than encouraging nature's protection simply for its right to be. Nature has already supplied an array of necessary elements to humans for survival. Should we not also work to ensure the survival of nature? That is the basis for

MAKING A LIVING

reciprocity. The right for organisms to exist unmolested and have adequate, healthy land, water, or sky in which to do so wasn't really a line of thought that was getting us far enough, fast enough to inspire business practices yielding positive results for nature in a scalable manner. And those two-by-fours supporting all of us have been weakening. In a way I'm still selling nature and the idea of developing new types of partnerships based on the benefits it provides to humans. It's our starting line. However, now I include reciprocity with nature as an additional goal to share space and resources with those superstars of structure, processes, and systems.

Now I'm teaching students and business leaders about nature's genius, a term coined by Janine Benyus in the late 1990s, and the mutual benefits all of us, humans and nonhumans alike, can derive from humans observing and adopting the strategies other organisms use as integral features of our businesses. After all, Lotusan® and the bullet train both ultimately require less energy and materials to do their jobs. This is absolutely good for business and benefits our natural resources too. But to get to the heart of this approach, please think further about the difference between being or serving a consumer versus being or serving a citizen concerned with the broader well-being of friends, society, nature, and the world in general.

When I was younger, my dad carefully and repeatedly told me business and making a living are what drives society. Ever-increasing production, profits, and overall growth were what we were all taught to embrace. Being productive, according to Dad, meant being successful in business first. Caring for the environment could come afterward as a luxury based on the bounty of one's bottom line. But what if caring and profiting could be reconciled – or at least made more compatible, I thought? What of reciprocity? Of citizenship?

Recently, I learned of a college instructor who asked his students how many of them were consumers.[4] Every person raised a hand. When he asked how many of them were citizens, he saw a few hands sparsely dotting the room. As he pursued this point in discussion, certain values emerged. The students' opinions seemed to converge on a common theme. In order to make a living under a consumer-driven model, the producer gains the "right" to deploy any means necessary to bring prices into the consumer's range of acceptance. However, a citizen-driven model encompasses a broader notion of responsibility to the whole. And in case citizen itself is too narrow or loaded a term in today's vernacular, we can extend it beyond specific countries toward a place of planetary belonging by using the term "global citizen." Certainly we all belong here. A global citizen-driven model honors the dollar, but only as part of a larger construct. This model contains love and culture, and takes into account the collective well-being of fellow global citizens and nature both for its many offerings to people of course – but also nature simply for itself. This is what makes sense to me – a world extending beyond what we buy and sell. This is why, several decades ago, I started searching for people inside companies who perform their work as global citizens – and help their companies in the process. And then one day I picked up Janine's book, *Biomimicry: Innovation Inspired by Nature*,[5] and found a new way of doing business successfully that utilized the two-by-fours mutually supporting humans and other living organisms and systems.

So, how have biomimicry and related practices found their way into successful companies where they (or some version of them) are being used? Those of us wanting to see biomimicry utilized further in business have been asking the question, "How do we get biomimicry into business?" This, as it turns out, is the wrong question. The question should have been all along, "How are businesses using biomimicry already?" Of course, this is usually followed in rapid-fire succession by additional questions such as the following:

How are businesses experiencing success or failure with biomimicry and its related but importantly distinct methodologies?

Are they applying biomimetics to their products or processes? To material sourcing and/or acquisition?

How was biomimicry introduced into the company?

Can the principles of biomimicry be scaled up and if so, how? If not, why not and does that take away from existing successes?

Where are the speed bumps for adoption and integration of biomimicry into companies?

Through my work teaching biomimicry, I discovered biomimicry has many faces, many cousins, and many entry points into the workplace. It can be introduced head-on as full-blown biomimicry not only emulating nature's genius organisms but conforming to the underlying physical, chemical, and biological requirements of Earth in order to solve specific problems in innovative ways. It can also be one of a suite of tools used to make particular products or processes successful. It can guide a design process from a new product's beginnings or come in midway or even late in a business's development or operations process to enhance an endeavor already on its way to market. Each of these methods of adoption can yield a positive *triple bottom line* where benefits are attained in profit as well as for planet and people.

With any pioneering process or product, replicability and scaling up are critical goals. However, if the totality of its value isn't specifically measured – and often with biomimicry it hasn't been – companies may not realize the scale of value or, indeed, that there is any real value at all in using it regularly versus using another sustainability practice. This begets another question: Are the results or value of biomimicry measured in the companies that use it? If so, how? If not, why?

And finally, what form of reciprocity will emerge from the adoption of biomimicry? Will companies work as the Sto Corporation and designers of the Shinkansen train have by engaging in a simple transaction of emulating structures found in nature resulting in the use of fewer resources and reduction of harmful outputs? These are excellent accomplishment in and of themselves. But what more could we do? How could we deepen these partnerships into the realm of reciprocity?

So many questions. As you continue to read, you'll find the backstories of how biomimicry came into use and to what end by very different kinds of companies at different stages of growth and development. When you finish these portraits, you will read some of the lessons learned by each company. A portion of those lessons are revealed simply from the stories or the innovators themselves. Others are excerpted from actual business case studies conducted by Jacques Chirazi and his colleagues at the Biomimicry Advisory Group. Some companies answer, it would seem, all of these questions; others just a few of the ones most important to them. Biomimicry is not one-size-fits-all.

You'll also likely notice many similar personality and "action" traits of the various business leaders you meet in the following pages, but also differences. For some, the decision to use biomimicry sprang from company leaders' innate desire to follow nature's rules and strategies – to be more respectful to Earth as they harvested profits. Others bit into a concept they instinctively knew would work. Then they acted persistently and inventively enough to leap all the hurdles required in order to capitalize on innovations in which they absolutely believed. Still others thumbed their noses at convention and just bulled through the challenges to successfully integrate innovations into the workplace. They have all worked in their own ways.

The companies in the following pages have set their feet upon the road toward reciprocity with other living organisms by learning from and respecting their nonhuman strategies while reducing human impact on the environment. In some cases, that road was seemingly easy and straightforward for the practitioner. Sometimes the path had a few more twists and turns. Company leaders and employees in these five successful companies and an increasing cadre have created partnerships fusing business and strategies learned from observing and emulating nature. In the process, these business professionals have created change that has yielded reductions in material and energy use, reductions in waste streams, and reductions in use or creation of harmful chemicals. The strategies contained in designs or processes they found in nature are also helping them put bread on the table by making a profit. Their teachers are not other humans, but the oldest professor of all – nature itself.

More and more businesses are connecting the dots and surmounting the obstacles to these innovations as well as learning and applying the steps to achieve biomimicry. By asking, "What would nature do?" or "How does nature solve this problem?" while adhering to good business practices, an ever greater number of companies are experiencing success. In the businesses storied here, results were and are positive for the company's bottom line, the people in the company, their clients, and the planet. For those of us global citizens going to work to make a living while working toward reciprocity, these are worthy tools to use.

REFERENCES

1 United States Department of Agriculture. "U.S. Forest Resource Facts and Historical Trends." https://www.fia.fs.fed.us/library/brochures/docs/2012/ForestFacts_1952-2012_English.pdf. Accessed 18 August, 2016.

2 Tallamy, Doug. "20 Most Valuable Woody and Perennial Native Plant Genera in Terms of Supporting Biodiversity in the Mid-Atlantic Region."

10 MAKING A LIVING

University of Maryland Department of Environmental Science & Technology. http://enst.umd.edu//sites/enst.umd.edu/files/_docs/Table%201%20from%20Doug%20Tallamy%20Sheet1.pdf. Accessed 9 September, 2016.

3 Biomimicry 3.8. "Life's Principles Design Lens." https://biomimicry.net/the-buzz/resources/designlens-lifes-principles/. Accessed 3 March, 2016.

4 Downton, Paul. "Straw Polls, Dodos and the Value of Landscape." *The Nature of Cities.* https://www.thenatureofcities.com/2013/03/31/straw-polls-dodos-and-the-value-of-landscape/. Accessed 31 May, 2016.

5 Benyus, Janine. *Biomimicry: Innovation Inspired by Nature.* New York, NY: Harper Perennial, 1997.

ON MOUNTAIN GOATS AND CITIZENSHIP – THE NIKE STORY OF BIOMIMICRY

I would feel more optimistic about a bright future for man
if he spent less time proving that he can outwit Nature
and more time tasting her sweetness and respecting her seniority.[1]

E. B. White

Adventure racing and other all-terrain human-powered pursuits had become more than just another fad by the late 1990s, and Nike was working to deliver a stellar cross-country shoe. A company known for performance and responsiveness, Nike had advance product teams considering targeted ways to improve shoe performance in challenging terrains across creeks, over rock ledges, and through the woods. As they were mulling over the various landscapes humans were attempting to master, the discussion turned to the adroit hoof work of mountain goats.

Mountain goats spend their lives, literally, on the face of a rock. Survival in their vertical world depends on strength, balance and those amazing hooves. When clambering over steep, rocky terrain, two factors give goats a leg up when it comes to feet – rigid exterior support and friction.

Goat feet are split into halves resulting in cloven hooves. Each hoof houses a stiff exterior wall and a soft, pliable sole. The combination allows goats to balance on their hoof edges as they pick their way across impossibly thin ledges on rock outcroppings or smear the central soles of their hooves on steep, smooth inclines, allowing friction to hold them on the mountainside. Recognizing this advantage,

Mike Friton and other innovators at Nike did their best to integrate those features into a shoe featuring a mechanism they then named Goat Tek. At some point, one of the team members had to ask, "How do goats do it?" *Looking to nature to supply an answer to their challenge gave them their next shoe.*

Why did the designers look to nature for the answer to this question? In the broadest sense, outdoor shoe designers are required to consider the outdoors. Usually, they are people who have spent a good deal of time there pursuing their hobbies, and they have an affinity for, if not nature, at least for being out in it.

If we were to put a name to this attraction to the outdoors, we might opt for *biophilia*. Biophilia literally means a love of life and the living world. With its roots in evolutionary psychology and sociocultural theory biophilia, at its core, is the idea that humans feel an important affinity for or tie to other living things and living systems. Benefits of biophilia extend beyond the simple enjoyment of the outdoors as a place to relax and play though. As Florence Williams recently noted in her book, *The Nature Fix*, researchers are finding measurable benefits of being in natural settings such as decreases in cortisol and blood pressure as well as increases in creativity.[2] So in addition to acknowledging benefits of being out in nature based on this love or connection to nature, there are health benefits to consider in the workplace as well. But that simple love of and affinity for nature alone may account for the wonder we feel as we observe the amazing feats of creatures like mountain goats, leading us to consider and copy their gifts.

It is exactly that copying which throws the Nike group somewhat over the fence into the field of bio-inspiration and eventually into the first layers of biomimicry. Originally coined by Otto Schmitt in the 1950s, biomimicry was defined as the "study of biological formation, structure and function along with the materials, mechanisms and processes for the purposes of mimicking them."[3] In addition to emulating other living things, modern biomimicry designs have evolved to incorporate larger underlying natural patterns such as being "locally attuned and responsive" and "adapting to changing conditions."[4] This attention to patterns in nature extends the design process beyond mere mimicry into exploring the underlying reasons for why and how organisms do what they do. If a living thing is "attuned" to its local environment, it has the opportunity to more efficiently form feedback loops for procuring resources and utilizing waste. It can optimize for such things as light and precipitation, wind and pressure. If it can be responsive to those pressures and opportunities, it gives itself the best possibility for a long and productive life. Further, when local conditions change and the organism can adapt in a more long-term way to those changes, mimicking that organism's strategies can lead businesses to resilience and truly being able to reduce waste, use more earth-friendly processes, and increase efficiency without added materials or fuel. By deploying the biomimetic process as a starting block for inspiration and as a marker for evaluating the product, a company's product development needle can shift from simply enhancing performance for profit into the realm of using fewer natural resources and more life-friendly practices. In other words, their business model can evolve from strict consumerism into global citizenship. But when the Nike "Goat Tek" team first mimicked the mountain goat, it was just in service of building a better shoe.

Before Nike could fully attain and embrace biomimicry, two more elements were required: The first was Darcy Winslow. The second was profit.

In the mid-1990s, Darcy, an astute businesswoman with a quick smile, was working in product development spending a lot of time in Nike's various factories and supplier facilities around the world. During a sweltering summer in Thailand, she found herself walking by a factory work station where midsoles were attached to outsoles. The heavy odor in the thick air included volatile organic compounds (VOCs) emitted from that process. When she saw a visibly pregnant woman on the line, she approached her interpreter, "Can you ask her if the smell bothers her?" The answer shocked Darcy.

The woman said, "Only on Sundays." It was the one day she wasn't around the process. That was when she would get headaches.

Troubled, when Darcy returned to the states, she told the story to Nike's head chemist, Dick Crosbie. Although she didn't think this alone prompted the resulting actions in his department, timing was ripe for conversion. He started experiments with water-based adhesives instead of solvent-based ones – a shift he and Darcy hoped would sharply reduce or eliminate VOCs. It was definitely the shift that moved them from bio-inspiration into biomimicry.

In nature, except for some substances used in predation, chemistry is based around life-friendly models. Life-friendly chemistry is one of the basic markers for how nature conducts business. Even in cases of venoms or poisons emitted by organisms, such materials do no harm to the host plant or animal and are, by and large, water-soluble. When considering water-based adhesives, life-friendly chemistry and structures abound. Mussels adhere to rocks without negative results to either. Geckos climb vertical surfaces without emitting harmful substances. By mimicking the marker of water solubility, Nike truly began practicing biomimicry. By 1999 the company's move away from VOCs and toward life-friendly water-based adhesives may not have been absolute, but the percentages were in the high 90s.

That alone would not have been enough to change the young Thai woman's life, however. The factory was arranged so that shoe lines from a number of companies ran adjacent to each other through the plant. Nike could have reduced their VOCs to zero and not made an appreciable difference in the air she breathed.

"One line would be making Nike," Darcy recalled.

> The line right next to it would be making Adidas and then Reebok and then Avia. So, all of the companies were in the same manufacturing facility. Once we perfected the water-based compound, Dick Crosbie and the chemists at Nike came to agreement and pulled together all the other competitive brands' chemists to share that technology. That was our first experience with giving away any new technology.

That was the day the sneaker crossed the line from a consumer-oriented model to a more global citizen-oriented one through care for the greater good.

Before that event, Nike didn't share anything, nor did anyone else in the sport shoe market – a basic theory of competitive advantage dictated against giving innovation secrets away. Over time, however, Nike and its competitors came to understand the tragedy of the commons – that each acting in their own best interests individually might diminish their larger community because human or natural resources could end up being harmed or depleted for all of them if they continued on that path. They began talking more about important problems outside competitive advantage and brand uniqueness – problems facing the entire industry like human and environmental health.

As the company continued to evolve, Darcy began overseeing Global Research Design and Development where the Goat Tek team had done its work. Partially because of that young woman's plight and partly because she was now seeing signs of and logic in sustainability everywhere, Darcy started working on a sustainability framework for Nike. She had developed 2020 goals for sustainability when she approached Nike's president and CEO saying, "If we're going to be serious about sustainability it's got to happen within the context of business – not just in corporate responsibility. We don't create policy. We create products."

Leadership told her to figure it out. She had no team, no budget, no title. There was just a vision to achieve these 2020 sustainability goals. Her role was to continue working with inside teams as well as other companies to achieve those goals through a new internal group called sustainable business strategies.

There, they examined as many different ways to think about sustainability as they could, knowing that no one framework could answer all of their questions. No one language applies to all the different functions. They brought in programs and ideas from Cradle to Cradle and the Natural Step. They studied design chemistry and poured over Donella Meadows's systems thinking work.

Then at a Natural Step Conference in 2000, a group of about 200 people were going through the requisite, "I'm so-and-so from such-and-such and work for x company." Darcy was bracing herself for a long session when a young woman up front said, "Dayna Baumeister – biomimicry – Missoula, Montana." When the session was over, the two met and talked for hours.

Shortly after, Darcy brought Dayna to speak to a group of about 20 people from 20 different departments at Nike. Their roles ranged from design and manufacturing to finance and transportation. It was important, Darcy thought, to see where biomimicry resonated within the company – and where it didn't. She wasn't surprised when the designers, the "creatives" in the group, latched onto the concept.

What followed was a series of 15–20 workshops with Dayna and her business partner, Janine Benyus who, in addition to writing, cofounded the Biomimicry Guild, now Biomimicry 3.8 (or B3.8 as we'll refer to them) with Dayna. They taught the group the essentials of biomimicry, teased out challenges the company was facing, and then worked with them to find potential strategies from nature's genius organisms to emulate.

Since Nike had already engaged in basic biomimicry by mimicking the structure of goat hooves, the idea of asking, "How does nature do that?" came easily. In fact, it came much more easily than did other sustainability techniques as it was and is driven by questions instead of the ominous "Thou shalt not's" employees confronted elsewhere.

One of the first challenges they delved into more deeply seemed natural considering this was the birthplace of "Nike Air." It was the question How does nature cushion? They began addressing their 20-year sustainability goals through the lens of biomimicry. How does nature cushion without creating waste? In a closed-loop system?[5] The group started to learn the difference between the more shallow mimicry of structure and form, and deeper mimicry which emulates processes and systems all working toward creating life-friendly conditions. They then plunged into that question – How does nature stick things together without toxins? In addition to their prior experience addressing specific product innovations, biomimicry opened up a whole new array of inspirational tools to move away from problems with solvent-based adhesives and use of traditional rubber. In roughly three years, Nike replaced the approximate 147 chemicals in the latter, many of which were toxic. They were able to remove all the toxic chemicals coining the result "green rubber."

Nature's array of tools for sticking one thing to another at room temperature and pressure without harmful chemicals is a challenge present in many business applications. Within Nike alone, "stickiness" was a challenge faced in a number of departments, and a variety of natural models were considered. One of the most talked about models Nike and a number of businesses examined for tackling that particular problem was gecko feet.

The undersides of gecko toes are covered with hundreds of thousands of hairlike filaments extending from the surfaces – each of those with split ends. Because any object has a microscopic "attraction" to other objects, the sheer force of the number of these projections allows for enough attraction to enable geckos to scramble up seemingly traction-less surfaces like walls and even windows. Another effective example revolves around starfish and octopi who have the help of dimpled suction cup-shaped "feet" to help them gain traction. Frogs and similarly equipped creatures capitalize on moisture emitted from their toes to gain a hold on surfaces. You may have used a similar moisture-based strategy while leafing through the pages of what you're currently reading.

With all these strategies available for potential solutions to advance materials and practices, Nike decided to upgrade its design library – one of the most revered places at the company. With Dayna helping the librarian and creative group, the library was transformed into a biomimicry museum of sorts. Available to everyone, the library became one of the most inspiring places on the entire Nike campus.

During that same period of time, Nike hired one of B3.8's Biologists at the Design Table (BaDT). BaDTs are available to consult with any company to help translate nature's genius into problem-solving products and processes. As important, these consultants work with an array of professionals – biologists, designers, and engineers – all of whom are necessary to bring biomimetic advances to profitable fruition. The BaDT working with Nike took the group through brainstorming sessions, presentations, and problem-solving discussions to attack some of the company's knottiest problems.

This was an exciting time, but Darcy knew she needed more than a once-in-time series of visits to integrate biomimicry into the company. She was searching for the tipping point which would cement the practice into the workplace. It was during this time she reflected on Bill McDonough's words, "Design is the first signal of human intention." She started knocking on the creatives' doors, knowing she needed to get at least 20% of the group moving with her to really soak biomimicry and sustainability in general into the design machine.

"We had somewhere between 22,000 and 24,000 people working in about a hundred countries around the world. If I could get 20% of the most influential creatives, designers and innovators on board – then we had a chance at building some momentum."

Although it depended on the day, who it was, and what other stress points they were dealing with at the time – Darcy, armed with 3×5 cards listing the biomimetic "Nine Laws of Nature,"[6] on one

18 THE NIKE STORY OF BIOMIMICRY

side, and "Places to Intervene in a System,"[7] on the other, was inde-fatigable.

> One of my workmates noticed the ability to become multi-lingual was critical to gaining acceptance. If you were speaking to a CFO you used one language with creatives, another. It had become our job to be that translator.

Thinking about the tipping point, Darcy began to explore opportunities that might exist in the Human Relations department. Nike didn't really hire biologists, but if they could create a database of employees who had biological training in their background, Darcy knew they might be able to integrate biomimicry into their systems. Employees with biological training had the language and methodologies to make sure biomimicry tools continued to be used.

> We really started to tap into them as a kind of lightning rod when these kinds of questions would come up. I think something like that could be easily implemented in any company.

More challenges came in dealing with company cycles. Outdoor wear companies market their products to customers based on the four seasons, and each new product has an overall cycle of 18 months from concept to retail. Between the product cycles and new employees, Nike was challenged to translate biomimicry to those who hadn't been part of the movement when biomimicry was first introduced. Still, the practice had lodged itself in the company psyche in at least two important ways.

Darcy recalled, "Our materials group – advanced materials research and sourcing – was another group where biomimicry resonated and to this day I think a lot of the work resides there."

Discussing the chemists, she noted the second element cementing biomimicry into the company.

> As to the green rubber, it actually turned out to be less expensive. That had an impact on our bottom line. In the early stages of this work we calculated how much waste material was created on average each year and per pair of shoes. When we started, for each pair of shoes we made, there was a third shoe's equivalent in

THE NIKE STORY OF BIOMIMICRY **19**

waste. So, we used to walk around with the material waste from one pair of shoes and say, 'See, this is what's getting incinerated and landfilled in somebody's backyard.'

When that failed to get sufficient attention we analyzed how much it was worth. In 1999 when we first did the calculations, that waste was valued at upwards of $700 million worth of materials being landfilled or incinerated just in our footwear business. That got their attention.

Money is a critical motivator for change, but there was one other element of biomimicry that had huge impact and staying power within the company. As Nike packed their toolbox to create the lightest, fastest, and highest performing sport shoes, the focus on biomimicry also imbued people in the company with the power of global citizenship – a sense of caring for people and nature in concert with the bottom line.

As she reflected on its impact Darcy remembered,

> Many people interpreted sustainability as us coming in as the police – you can't do this or you can't do that. What biomimicry allowed us to do was to say – "Look at this whole world that you can now tap into. It's always been there, but let's look to nature for its 3.8 billion years of R&D and ask how it would accomplish the same tasks we have in this company." So, instead of closing doors, we opened up a huge door for the company and its employees to enter and begin to explore.

It also gave employees a new lens with which to see the world and participate – as global citizens.

At the same time, men and women in Thailand were breathing healthier air and a mountain goat on a distant spire leapt across a great divide.

NIKE LESSONS LEARNED

Nike has played all around the arena of biomimicry and its relatives. They created bioinspired shoes like the Mercurial Superfly 360 which were once adorned with cheetah-like spots. Although they mimicked color alone in that shoe, designers later transitioned to the more biomimetic Goat Tek which imitated the hoof structure of its natural mentor. As they moved forward, the company imbued employees with the power of global citizenship by combining goals benefitting profit, planet, and people by creating high-performing, well-made shoes out of "green rubber." Using water-based solvents, they progressed into emulating life-friendly chemical processes while enhancing the work environment of those on the production line, air quality, and the bottom line simultaneously. In all this, Nike has lived their quote to "Change the game." Here are some of the lessons Nike has learned in its dive into bio-inspiration and biomimicry.

There doesn't have to be a single inciting incident to begin using biomimicry. In Nike's case, designers used cheetah spots as a color scheme to serve as early bio-inspiration to create a marketing metaphor for speed. Later, product engineers dove deeper by imitating structure. And management raised a flag for chemists based on observations in distant manufacturing plants, which ignited the search for and discovery of benign chemical processes – cutting waste in the process. *Bio-inspiration and biomimicry can arise in many places within a company.*

They also learned biomimicry can be applied at multiple levels. Color, structure, processes, and even systems can be improved by emulating nature. As an example of this systems approach, the acacia tree provides food and shelter for ants who then return the favor by biting would-be plant eaters and in some cases even inhibiting disease. This system is comprised of a series or set of organism products and behaviors – working synergistically together. Likewise, Nike chemists shared intellectual property. They found when they developed and shared water-based solvents in a cooperative manner to advance their goals of protecting line workers, they became better corporate global citizens in the process. In doing this, Nike found they not only solved their glue challenges but also created happier, healthier employees.

Companies, like nature, must adapt to survive. Although they may not have gleaned this one from nature, those multiple levels of mimicry we just discussed are not simply destinations. They can and should serve as springboards for adaptation and innovation. Nike staff learned a company can begin by mimicking in one way, such as cushioning without toxins, then realize further benefits including financial savings by taking that innovation into new forms of emulation such as recognizing and studying the ways nature eschews waste.

By adapting and fitting form to function, the company worked to curb excess from within, thereby reducing that "third shoe" bit of waste and saving $700 million in the process.

Since nature runs on information and exhibits optimization over maximization,[8] *Darcy knew she had to communicate biomimicry to a critical mass of people within the company.* She felt like she needed at least 20% of Nike's employees engaged in biomimicry in order for it to stick – and she wanted it to stick. Purposefully presenting the methodology to a wide array of employees and then zeroing in on the designers and innovators worked well for two reasons: First, looking to nature for problem-solving strategies seemed to resonate with these people. She knew that interest would help her influence a larger sector of the company. The second reason she was enthusiastic about the interest this particular collection of employees exhibited was that if they could begin the design process with the intent to do better for the environment and the employees as well as the clients and profits, they were more likely to hit their ultimate triple bottom-line mark. That level of intention would have been approved of by the baseball great, Yogi Berra, who set the stage for McDonough by suggesting, "If you don't know where you are going, you'll end up someplace else."

Another way she worked to deploy the practices was to seek out employees who already had some biology training in their backgrounds. *Like nature, she was locally attuned and used readily available resources.*[8] But she also recognized the value of bringing in professionals who used biomimicry regularly. She brought in trained BaDT from B3.8 to work with her team. As they began to work further with the meme, she assisted staff in the vital step of becoming multilingual – translating from biology to design and engineering, then back again. Integrating new problem-solving platforms like biomimicry into a company requires employees to understand each other's professional languages with all their vocabulary, acronyms, and even operating practices. In a business of multiple seasonal production cycles, introduction, integration, and retention of new practices can be challenging. For that reason, and simply to up their innovation game, Darcy noted that were she to introduce biomimicry to the company today, she would begin the process in new employee orientation.

Regardless of where biomimicry is introduced within a company, *asking staff and colleagues questions – and getting them to ask further questions — is more powerful for innovative spaces than governing by "Thou shalt not's" to further sustainability goals.* This is why biomimicry is still being used and still evolving in the company. It's palatable.

And yet, embracing biomimicry, like any innovation, also relies on context. Is the innovation needed? Is the timing appropriate to the design development process? What else is going on? What are the opportunity costs and return-on-investment possibilities?

The context questions are ripe for any company, and Nike is still using biomimicry as a tool to meet its needs. Today, feedback loops are a new nature-inspired tool in their corral driving dozens of products on their current palette. And they're still asking, "How would nature do that?"

ACKNOWLEDGMENTS

Large portions of this chapter were taken from interviews between the author and Darcy Winslow in November of 2014. My thanks to Darcy for her story and willingness to share it are as large as the great outdoors.

REFERENCES

1 White, E. B. "The Coon Tree." *The New Yorker*, June 14, 1956.

2 Williams, Florence. *The Nature Fix.* New York, NY: W.W. Norton and Company, 2017.

3 Harkness, J. "In Appreciation of a Lifetime of Connections: Otto Herbert Schmitt, 1913–1998." *Physics in Perspective* 4 (2002), 456–490. https://doi.org/10.1007/s000160200005.

4 Biomimicry 3.8. "Life's Principles Design Lens." https://biomimicry.net/the-buzz/resources/designlens-lifes-principles/. Accessed 20 February, 2018.

5 Biomimicry Institute. https://biomimicry.org/. Accessed 11 July, 2018.

6 Benyus, Janine. *Biomimicry: Innovation Inspired by Nature.* New York, NY: Harper Perennial, 1997.

7 Meadows, Donella H. *Thinking in Systems: A Primer.* White River Junction, VT: Chelsea Green, 2008.

8 Biomimicry Institute. https://biomimicry.org/. Accessed 12 July, 2018.

WHAT IS BIOMIMICRY AND WHY USE IT?

To see things in the seed, that is genius.

Lao Tzu

Leonardo da Vinci carefully surveyed birds winging their way across the Italian sky. He studied their sleek lines and wing structures to learn the functional strategies which allowed them their lofty domain. As he did, he came up with ideas for how humans might fly using those same strategies. He was practicing an early form of problem-solving and design based on nature's ways of getting its many jobs done. Today we would primarily call what Leonardo practiced as he created conceptual drawings for flying machines and other such inventions, bio-inspiration. A great observer of nature, he examined not only mechanisms birds used to fly but also flight behaviors. He even went so far as to discuss and include his impressions on center of gravity, gravity itself, density, and motion associated with flying – even though many of the observations didn't pan out as fully functional solutions when he created his models.

The biomimicry we practice today has a few more steps but is still rooted in that early premise. After Leonardo, a procession of inventors observed and emulated nature, but the practice didn't really "stick" until a man named George de Mestral looked closely at the hooked barbs of burs clinging to his dog's fur after a hunting trip. Mimicking those hooks on one strip of fabric and pairing it with loops on another strip provided him with the intellectual property he needed to patent Velcro. He looked. He emulated. He flourished.

24   WHAT IS BIOMIMICRY AND WHY USE IT?

As you've read, Otto Schmitt later named and defined biomimetics as applying natural solutions to engineering problems, but it wasn't until a sandy-haired natural resource manager, Janine Benyus, wrote her seminal book[1] in 1997 that the word "biomimicry" became popularized. Janine then partnered with colleague Dr. Dayna Baumeister, and an entire profession sprang up around the practice of seeking out and reconnecting with nature to observe organisms for the purpose of creating new solutions for businesses. With biomimicry as their focus, they created the Biomimicry Guild, later dubbed B3.8 for the 3.8 billion years organisms have been developing strategies to build with stronger but lighter materials, transport goods in an energy-efficient way, keep things dry, keep things moist and a raft of other strategies valuable to them and – as it turns out – to us as well. They taught practitioners (dubbed biomimics) and business leaders to innovate, not through inspiration alone but by looking more deeply to how organisms interact with rules and deep patterns existing on Earth, then adapt strategies to succeed by operating within those frameworks. They began urging all these practitioners to consider and design solutions with humans as part of, not apart from, nature and all its components. This effort – biomimicry – has generated inventions like Nike's green rubber as well as whole system modifications which have created record profits in some businesses or entirely new companies all by emulating nature's structures, processes, and systems in the workplace. You can do this in your business too.

A handy place to begin with any venture, methodology, or concept is to learn the language used by the people who are already profiting by it. Darcy and Nike taught us that. Don't panic. To move forward effectively, we only have to look at six definitions of terms – those of biomimicry and its cousins.

MEET THE FAMILY

We'll start with the biophilia which led Nike's designers outside in the first place. As you read earlier, this word literally translates to "love of life" from the Greek *bios* or life and *philia* or love. Quite literally, it means *brotherly love* – worth mentioning since the Greeks had four different words for the emotion. As a sportswear and gear company, many of Nike's employees embrace being out in nature, literally loving the life, healthy air, and water around them. Being

WHAT IS BIOMIMICRY AND WHY USE IT?   **25**

outside, it is little wonder they pondered the attributes of various creatures accomplishing things like climbing mountains – things the designers also wished to do.

As we relate it to business, this love of living things is used by a broad array of professionals from designers to architects, landscapers, educators, and others who work to reconnect us to nature, its components, and its benefits. The practice often includes bringing plants directly into the workplace, not only in traditional planters for aesthetics but as sound-damping wallscapes, room dividers, and even snack zones where employees or tenants can harvest a bite to eat. However, the concept is really much more expansive than plants alone and extends to recreating the more organic flows found in nature into our everyday surroundings by upgrading office and building layouts as well as reconfiguring and modifying elements like furniture design. Applications of biophilia reconnect us with natural forces like water, outdoor light, and airflow as well as natural materials throughout offices, homes, and public spaces. These may manifest as traditional objects being used in new ways or as completely new building elements like waterfalls used as part of water filtration systems, window systems admitting light and air from nontraditional locations, and plant applications placed on interior walls to improve air quality or exterior walls to enhance work environments and/or subdue heat island effects in cities.

We can thank Erich Fromm and, more recently, E. O. Wilson for introducing the concept to us in modern times, but Aristotle talked about biophilia as far back as 300 B.C. underscoring the importance of our connections to nature. Biophilic design is used not only to please the senses but more and more to reduce stress[2] and fatigue,[3,4] enhance performance,[5] and, its practitioners would say (and I would agree), improve quality of life[6] wherever it takes root (if you'll pardon the pun). Over time, a growing collection of research is illustrating how this is accomplished and demonstrating new, productive ways to reconnect with the natural world we crave, whether we know it or not. Alright, that's enough for cousin number one – biophilia.

The second term we'll consider is bio-utilization, in which we engage some living organisms to help us accomplish a task. Examples of bio-utilization range broadly and can include everything from using dogs to help us herd sheep to planting trees to shelter our

26   WHAT IS BIOMIMICRY AND WHY USE IT?

homes from wind and sun. More recently, we have widened our bio-utilization practices to achieve more complex tasks. Algae are now being investigated as potential biofuels and for uses such as thickening agents in cosmetics. Ecovative Design creates packaging out of living fungi. In my own nascent biomimicry work, I partnered with colleagues to design a wastewater treatment facility partially powered by bacteria to help us remove pollutants from water. Of course, since we were aiming toward biomimicry, this bio-utilization portion of the design missed our particular mark – but that exact practice is used broadly now as of the larger, more complex operating systems in wastewater treatment facilities today. So, bio-utilization, using nature to help us complete tasks, will stand as our cousin number two.

Bionics is the practice of observing, translating, and applying organism abilities into technological solutions. Many times, but not always, professionals apply bionics to devices operating in concert with the body – primarily for challenges *to* the body. By studying how organisms walk, run, listen, see, and even think; inventors are helping people accomplish all those functions when their own bodies are unable to do so.

Massachusetts Institute of Technology (MIT) researcher Hugh Herr lost both his legs in a mountain-climbing accident, but instead of resigning himself to a wheelchair, he studied how feet and legs operated. In his shop at home, he began carving new feet specifically shaped for climbing to operate in an optimized manner for that particular sport. Later, as a researcher for MIT, he began working on inventions which ultimately helped him and other amputees walk and even dance again. The next landscape he turned his attention to was helping others by conceiving or inventing articles which can be attached to or implanted into the body – or even grown on their own and later integrated into individuals to help them live fulfilling lives. Cousin number three – bionics.

A more distant cousin is the methodology labeled BioTRIZ. Many problems in work (or really life in general) become apparent when underlying contradictions are identified. Theory of Inventive Problem Solving (TRIZ) practitioners observe when one problem is solved for, another becomes worse. TRIZ partially resolves this dilemma through use of Inventive Principles derived from studying patents shown to address these contradictions. BioTRIZ is a technological blending of some biology with those original TRIZ elements. Use of a matrix then allows solution seekers to collectively blend engineering axioms, rules of biology, and management elements to consider components such as substance, structure, space, time, energy, and information– all to form a solution.

Biomimicry's fifth and closer relative is bio-inspiration. Bio-inspiration is a process through which a person observes something in nature, which then stimulates an idea for solving a problem. Modern airplanes have been inspired by the flight of birds. Propulsion systems for watercraft have been inspired by the jetlike water propulsion of octopus. Spiders have inspired the design of robots with capabilities to go into places too hazardous for humans to tread. Even mountain goats lent a hoof toward design.

It is worth noting that bio-inspiration isn't carried out with the exact strategies organisms apply nor does it necessarily comply with nature's deep patterns. In fact, bio-inspiration can be extracted simply from very focused application of specific biomechanical or biological actions or processes. A good example is the ultracane, a helpful device for sight-impaired individuals. Inspired by the echolocation bats use both to avoid obstacles and to target food, the cane uses sonar to detect objects in front of and even somewhat above the user. However, instead of bouncing off the item and straight back to an ear, which immediately allows bats to adjust course, signals bounce back to a receiver and are then transferred to buttons on the cane which create a vibrating buzz. The thumb of the hand carrying the cane feels the buzz, and the user is alerted to the presence of an obstacle along with its relative height. While this innovative device is helpful to humans, bat sonar communicates not only the presence of an object but its size, speed, and direction of travel. As we are able to study bats further, we will learn more of their specific guidance strategies – allowing us to refine our own bioinspired tools even further.

Since the extensive use of biomimicry is still so new, many biomimetic inventions have been confused with a number of the cousins you've just met – and vice versa. Biomimics have fretted over this to greater or lesser degrees, and the vocabulary challenge may have hindered the application of biomimicry in some ways. Nature's forms did bioinspire an array of Leonardo's inventions, but the methods he used and the underlying science available to him at that time did not allow him to pass into the realm of biomimicry – which he undoubtedly would have had he lived today. Still, biomimicry is sometimes ascribed to his work. Biomimetics feels like it should mean the overall practice of biomimicry, but professionals from different parts of the world use that particular word to mean different things. We should be gentle with ourselves for sometimes intermixing these terms – even as much as we should also be mindful of their differences and similarities. Professionals working in these arenas are continually working to clarify and further segregate their meanings.

In the meantime, it is also important to understand there is no formal hierarchy of greatness among these practices. They are all remarkable for what we can accomplish when using them or even a blend of the methodologies. In fact, recently in a work group comprised of practitioners from the Americas and Europe, the term biom★ emerged to serve in those situations where more than one of the cousins were being pressed into service at once.

Biomimicry itself is a straightforward term. *Bios* you already know. *Mimesis* means "to imitate"; thus, *to imitate life*. So, what else makes this different from its cousin bio-inspiration and the others? There are several elements which really do set biomimicry apart. Even though the practice is maturing and being used somewhat differently in various points around the globe, here I will borrow broadly from Janine's book, the consulting firm B3.8,[7] and the Biomimicry Institute[8] to create our definitional framework. It's hard to know where my knowledge and their teachings begin and end, so I'm simply going to credit them collectively as the originators of the terms and modes of operation in this section of the book. From the initial writing of Janine's book to the inception and growth of the two organizations she helped build and guide, biomimicry has continued to evolve. For that reason, and to make the term and its current practice most understandable, I will use words and concepts birthed along the timeline of this evolution to create the clearest view of the practice. Hopefully, this will inform subsequent ideas you may have on how you might use biomimicry in your own work today.

"Life creates conditions conducive to life," say Janine and the many of the practitioners using this tool. Organisms – be they plant, animal (us included), bacteria, or whatnot – have an innate desire or instinct to continue their species whether they are single-celled diatoms dancing in a pond, ferns finessing spores out into the forest air,

WHAT IS BIOMIMICRY AND WHY USE IT? **29**

or mammals producing nourishment for their offspring. Within all the settings where these processes take place, what is created comes about chemically, physically, and/or biologically through the parent organism that generated it in the first place. Then, as the new organism grows, it finds support from the surrounding natural systems which allow it to garner its food, water, shelter, and space in the proper arrangement for it to grow, prosper, and eventually itself reproduce. It manages all this in the ambient temperatures and pressures around it with a limited array of elemental building blocks.

"But," you may argue, "I am not trying to create life. I'm trying to build a better widget." Here's the challenge though. As we build our widgets, we require some form of the raw materials we discussed earlier. In our production process, we may have to cut away excess to form our widget, add chemicals to create the final materials, or preserve those materials. We may currently be required to apply heat or pressure or cold to mold the widget into the final form we desire. And most certainly, we create waste. But we can do better at less cost to us, our businesses, and the world around us. When nature creates conditions conducive to life, it takes into account all of the conditions present on Earth (think gravity for example) and all of the deep local patterns (one of several is material availability). In this way, nature can create the optimal level of performance to allow an organism to live for the least amount of cost. Nature is simply a brilliant entrepreneur and business manager! So, how can you do that? How can you approach problem-solving with the intent to build not only a better widget but a better world − embracing the ethos of reciprocity as well as working in conjunction with other living organisms?

MIND THE RULES

First, consider all nature's existing rules or operating conditions, as B3.8 colleagues refer to them. These existing rules or conditions serve as background context for any solution-making we do − and everything else on Earth. We can't get around them most of the time, and when we try, the cost can be great. Without Darcy's persuasive actions, their company would still be paying out $700 million in material waste, and workers would still be breathing harmful volatile organic compounds.

And everywhere on Earth, these conditions exist. Leaves fall to the ground because of gravity whether in Tennessee or Thailand. Even our muscles retain their strength partially because gravity requires muscle mass in order to move our bodies from place to place.

Another earthly requirement is sun power for the great majority of systems that feed us and all the organisms around us. This begins with the photosynthetic processes going on in plants and their kin who not only feed us but also process CO_2 and produce oxygen. The sun also warms the planet and everything on it. Part of the beauty of this is the engine it creates to power the water cycle. The warmth of the sun causes water to evaporate which creates clouds. When water collects in the clouds in sufficient amounts, it is then redistributed on Earth via precipitation. The presence and service of water and cyclic processes like the one just described are actually both operating conditions on our planet.

The water cycle may be a good place to start when discussing those rotations, but it is by no means the only cycle on Earth. In fact, cycles are everywhere. We have calendar cycles consisting of days, weeks, months, years, and so on. We have the chemical cycles like the nitrogen cycle we learned in school. We seldom think of its importance, but our crops (and therefore food) rely on that cycle. Nitrogen is also a critical building block for amino acids and the very DNA making up our bodies.

Gravity, sunlight, water, cyclic processes – and limits and boundaries. We're not very good at recognizing and/or respecting this operating condition – not by a margin. Perhaps it is part of being human, but we're always testing limits and stretching boundaries. Still, there is an altitude above which we cannot breathe without an artificial source of oxygen. There is an ocean depth beyond which the pressure is so intense we cannot descend even with the most highly advanced submarines. Extreme cold and heat can eventually foil our human form, and of course, the absence of any of the previous operating conditions would cause our demise.

In business too, we have limits. We are constrained by human resource capacity, investment capital, and distribution channel restrictions along with adequate natural resources and an array of other limiting factors. All the while, everything is constantly in a state of flux or change – which is, of course, our last earthly rule.

That final rule or operating condition, dynamic nonequilibrium, rolls around the mouth. Rolling around, in fact, may be the best way to think of this concept. Any condition on Earth you might imagine is constantly changing because of the many forces acting on it over time. As it changes, it doesn't simply move in two dimensions like a pendulum, but in many different directions at different rates of speed like a ball rolling around in a bowl. Consider the seasons. We don't move in a straight line from winter's icy breath to the warm days of summer. Instead, we must run the gauntlet of spring. Days start getting longer. Earth starts to warm, but not at an even pace because of shading, snowpack, etc. Precipitation patterns shift. All of these things happen simultaneously, and all affect each other, which results in you walking out the door in short sleeves because it was so warm yesterday, only to turn around to run get your jacket. To paraphrase Heraclitus, the only constant is change. Not to argue with Heraclitus, but Earth's other operating conditions are all things we can expect to constantly deal with – in addition to change.

Whenever and wherever there are rules in a system, those governed by said rules accommodate them in different ways because they themselves have different individual attributes and requirements. However, not recognizing and working within these rules invariably costs us and those around us – whether in time, money, or well-being. We know the need for water is a rule of Earth. Cactus and camels both need to store water in the dry climates where they live, but they do so in very different ways. In fact, a plethora of organisms have the same needs as well as individual differences in size, shape, body covering, metabolism – the list is exhaustive. Because we have a similar need for water, even though we differ in so many ways, we eventually begin to seek patterns that can serve as the basis for principles common among all life forms.

PAY ATTENTION TO PATTERNS

Just as B3.8 and the Biomimicry Institute have identified and educated us about these operating conditions on Earth, they have also recognized certain principles[9] based on deep unifying patterns found in nature to accommodate these conditions. They make no claims these are the only principles. In fact, as we learn more about Earth and practice biomimicry to a greater degree, both organizations have

32 WHAT IS BIOMIMICRY AND WHY USE IT?

enhanced the way we describe these conditions and patterns to make them clear and reflective of our most recent understandings of life forms, processes, and systems.

In business as in nature, much of what needs to be accomplished boils down to specific functions. Like camels and cacti, sometimes our work requires us to accomplish a task like storing water. In our cities too, we often want to store or infiltrate water, but sometimes we want to filter or shed it. The number of functions we solve for in business – whether in a company or community – is staggering. Each particular function also has its own specific details and requirements. Nature meets these challenges by complying with those original operating conditions through a majority of the principles or deep patterns mentioned. It does this to keep individual organisms and the systems in which they reside accomplishing all their required functions, if imperfectly, at least better even than a well-oiled machine.

Let's take a closer look at Life's Principles[7]:

1 Use life-friendly chemistry.
2 Integrate growth and development.
3 Be locally attuned and responsive.
4 Be efficient with both materials and energy.
5 Adapt to changing conditions.
6 Evolve to survive.

Using life-friendly chemistry, structures or processes in nature are able to break down into benign components which are usually soluble in water. This is accomplished with the fewest elements necessary. As Dayna is fond of saying, "Just because the entire table of elements exists doesn't mean we have to use all of it. Other life forms utilize a significantly smaller subset of those elements, yet yield an incredible array of elegant molecules, materials and solutions."[10]

Nature also integrates development and growth by self-organizing and building from the bottom up. In the human body, cells make up organs which combine to create circulatory, skeletal nervous systems, and more. As an example outside our own bodies, think of a beehive with its modular hexagonal chambers. One might store food, but as a group they function as food storage, birthing chambers and nurseries – a veritable bee city – assuring the growth and continuation of the whole.

WHAT IS BIOMIMICRY AND WHY USE IT? **33**

In each of these examples, as the entity grows, it also becomes more complex. It is not, however, growing for the sake of growth. If this were the case, we might encounter a person over 20 feet tall. Such a person, by the way, would have a stomach requiring 4 liters of food to fill it. Imagine the impact of that on our food system! No, remember limits and boundaries? This includes the idea that nature doesn't maximize. It optimizes. In biggest vs. best, best is better.

Part of optimizing is being in sync with all that surrounds an organism. Nature uses both materials and energy it can readily, locally access and uses both in extremely efficient ways. When nature takes advantage of cycles as trees do when their leaves shed annually, they shift their food production process from photosynthesis to fertilizer. The fact that these fallen leaves provide nourishment for the trees and surrounding plants while sheltering insects means both the plants and the insects eventually become nourishment for other living things when their life cycles are complete. As this occurs, a sort of cooperation comes into being, and a high-level form of reciprocity is born along with it. Life nurtures life. Life, in fact, must nurture life to succeed.

And those oak trees, insects, bees, and human bodies are efficient – in terms of both energy and materials. The efficiency created by this leaf recycling, along with the cycling of every other living, then dying thing, highlights the value of repurposing as a strategy enhancing the effective business of nature. The cactus mentioned earlier also uses strategies that allow for multifunctionality. As one example, some types of cactus contract their roots and above ground structures to protect themselves from daily heat while reversing this by swelling to collect water when rains eventually arrive. Other cacti have evolved a zigzagged shape. This adaptation allows self-shading during scorching days and water storage as the structure swells in rainstorms, thus becoming more efficient as form follows function and is used in more than one way.

You may also notice adaptations also respond in accordance with what is happening around them and to them at any given time. Heraclitus would enjoy a conversation about how living things adapt to change in the most remarkable ways. Forests function as the lungs of our planet, but what happens when one species succumbs to disease or attack? The myriad of other species takes over that task so long as they are present. (This underscores the importance of humans practicing reciprocity – to provide support for as many species as possible.) Additionally, the dispersal of forest plants' seeds occurs over time allowing for both self-renewal and a kind of decentralization which creates a greater ability to handle change. All of these living things are constantly renewing themselves in an ever-shifting give and take with all the surrounding forest organisms and nonliving components. All operate in compliance with the overarching conditions present.

Although they adapt to their immediate context and conditions, organisms and their adaptations also evolve over time. What works persists. What doesn't passes on. Successful strategies are used in ways most efficient for each individual and species as a group. Along the way, they certainly will experience the unexpected, but the most successful species will incorporate mistakes and even use them long term to benefit their species.

As you continue to read the stories of Interface, PAX, Encycle, and Sharklet, you'll see how company leaders have used the strategies above by practicing biomimicry alone or in concert with some of its relatives in order to make better products – more efficiently, with life-friendly chemistry, incorporating diversity, and yes, even mistakes to yield more profitable companies and satisfied customers while reducing their impact on Earth.

REFERENCES

1 Benyus, Janine. *Biomimicry: Innovation Inspired by Nature.* New York, NY: Harper Perennial, 1997.

2 Chang C.-Y., and P.-K. Chen. "Human Responses to Window Views and Indoor Plants in the Workplace". *HortScience* 40, No. 3 (2005), 1354–1359.

3 Kaplan R., and S. Kaplan. *The Experience of Nature: A Psychological Perspective.* Cambridge, UK: Cambridge University Press, 1989.

4 Grahn, Patrik and Ulrika K. Stigsdotter. "The Relation between Perceived Sensory Dimensions of Urban Green Space and Stress Restoration." *Journal of Landscape and Urban Planning* 94 (2010), 264–275.

5 Browning, B., C. Garvin, C. Ryan, N. Kallianpurkar, L. Labruto, S. Watson, and T. Knop. "The Economics of Biophilia: Why Designing with Nature in Mind Makes Financial Sense". Terrapin Bright Green. https://www.terrapinbrightgreen.com/report/economics-of-biophilia/ 2014. Accessed 2 August, 2018.

6 Grinde, Bjørn, and Grete G. Pati. "Biophilia: Does Visual Contact with Nature Impact on Health and Well-Being?" *International Journal of Environmental Research and Public Health* 6 (2009), 2332–2343.

7 Biomimicry 3.8. https://Biomimicry.net. Accessed 2 August, 2018.

8 Biomimicry Institute. https://biomimicry.org/. Accessed 2 August, 2018.

9 Biomimicry 3.8. "Life's Principles Design Lens." https://biomimicry.net/the-buzz/resources/designlens-lifes-principles/. Accessed 3 August, 2018.

10 Baumeister D. (personal communication, January 23, 2018).

4

BUSINESS FROM THE WILD – INTERFACE, INC.

No man is an island,
Entire of itself.
Each is a piece of the continent,
A part of the main.

John Donne

John Donne writes of the inescapable connection among all humankind, and yet his poetry is eerily incomplete. What are humans without bird song in the spring? How can we consider ourselves independent from the food, medicine, housing, oxygen, and spiritual sustenance that wild organisms and spaces provide? Our relationship to the wild is not one of separation; we are "braided" together.[1] Even a worm does not stand alone. What hubris to treat the world as if humans can.

Biomimicry is a tool we can use in business to recreate those connections and perhaps even reconcile with the wild to a degree. As you have seen biologists, chemists, designers, engineers, and other business professionals are reconnecting to the wild with this tool by emulating organisms, and as you'll see – even ecosystems– using nature's forms, processes, and systems as muse, teacher, and template.

But to mimic nature, one must first observe organisms and the forces acting on them that create a *genius of place*,[2] that recipe of strategies that allows life not just to exist but to prosper in specific conditions unique to any geographic location. These strategies of the wild can allow us to comply with those life principles previously discussed to optimize material use, build with life-friendly chemistry, and adapt to varied levels of moisture, temperature, pressure, and even oxygen. This genius of place is not a human space alone but a larger shared blend of wildness and order that together comprises ecosystems and is interwoven with our lives. This braid of wild and nonwild exists in a tenuous balance because, too often, we have not adequately honored the genius of the wild and are seldom even sure how much wildness is enough to solve a problem or ensure a flourishing world. The practice of biomimicry ventures into new solution spaces that recognize the value of the wild, while igniting hope for ways of doing business that closely attend to that genius of place.

Here is the story of Interface, Inc.'s journey toward plaiting its nonwild existence to the wild right outside the door – reconnecting it to the main.

≈

David was frustrated. Ray Anderson, Chief Executive Officer (CEO) at Interface, Inc., the world's largest manufacturer of modular carpet tiles and his main client, had issued a new vision for the company regarding sustainability.

"If we're successful," Anderson stated to employees and contractors, "we'll spend the rest of our days harvesting yester-year's carpets and other petrochemically derived products, recycling them into new materials; converting sunlight into energy; with zero scrap going to the landfill and zero emissions into the ecosystem. And we'll be doing well… very well… by doing good. That's the vision."

David Oakey of Oakey Designs was prepping for a three-year contract with Interface when Ray decided the carpet company was going to become sustainable. A carpet company in an industry where waste and dependence on petrochemicals was the rule of business – and now, sustainable? What did that even mean?

"It took me probably a year and a half of struggling to understand sustainability in our context," mused Oakey. His business mind was besieged by this new world of sustainability, the nexus where planet and people gained equal standing with profit. Nature's cycles seemed incompatible with the industrial textiles world he had always known. That world was born not in the twentieth-century Industrial

Revolution but thousands of years earlier when Asian shepherds first sheared their flocks and covered their floors with wool. Their human interest in overcoming and utilizing elements of the wild for clothing, for home use, or as space for crops, grazing, and expansion of permanent communities led them to alter wild places in an ever-increasing trajectory in lieu of regularly existing in concert with them. Oakey hadn't yet considered the relevance to business of wild species and systems adapting and retooling themselves over millions of years.

David feared that Ray's vision of sustainability meant designing with natural materials, which he knew would be cost prohibitive. Moreover, David thought, "Natural fibers don't perform like synthetics and even if they did, the amount of, say, sheep, we would need in Georgia alone for a growing population and carpet demand is mind-boggling." Oakey just couldn't connect the move to environmental sustainability with the economic realities required for this billion-dollar company.

However, Ray was successful, brilliant, kind, holistic, and – in the marriage of restorative thinking to business – dogmatic. After coming away from a company-wide meeting, David knew he had to either be on board with Ray's ideas or leave the company and go somewhere else. Sustainability – in whatever form – was going to happen here.

Ray had grown up in rural Georgia, a place where fragmented wildlands persisted. He walked to ball practice surrounded by nature's cycles. Towering long leaf pines and Shumard oaks shading his footsteps hosted hawks with predatory focus on gray squirrels below. The squirrels, with watchful eyes and tails maniacally twitching, sported mouthfuls of Shumard bounty, while beetles systematically decimated the bodies of fallen oaks, returning them to earth. Cycles within cycles.

But Ray's younger days were more pressed toward success in football, school, and business than attending to the ecological cycles that make the world and the lives of all its harried, varied inhabitants possible. It wasn't until 1994, after reading Paul Hawken's[3] description of how humans have disrupted natural cycles and Daniel Quinn's[4] description of "givers" and "takers," that he was moved toward blending conservation with business leadership. And now, he was asking Oakey to do the same.

So while David pondered this new challenge, over at the Interface Innovation Department John Bradford, a farm boy who had added mechanical engineering to his resume, was breathing the satisfied breath of a businessman who has suddenly been freed to do better. As the Chief Innovation Officer at the time, John could now mesh his experiences from growing up on a farm with what he had learned as a mechanical engineer making carpet – shooting him forward onto the then mostly blank canvas of sustainability in business.

In the early days of sustainability at Interface, John noted, "We started to really dream about what it meant for the company in the product and process aspects and in the inspirational innovation side of the business." John reflected on the times, "We started to really teach [the team], you know? Everybody read the same books. Everybody studied how to apply different streams of sustainable thought into different parts of the business."

Their Director of Innovation, Bill Jones, said it began simply "with the idea of using less and wasting less." Bill was working in the factory as the ideas started taking hold:

> We'd been working with polylactic acid and continuously having struggles over the performance, availability, price, flexibility and tenacity of the yarn. Then, we introduced a product with high post-industrial recycled content and achieved a 40% reduction on all seven measurements used in Life Cycle Assessment.

Bill realized, "You're doing this! This is great!"

But simply reducing use of materials is not how nature manages or how it heals after disruption. It also wasn't Ray's idea of success. To adhere to nature's principles – to become restorative by reconciling manufacturing practices with nature's wild guidance – the company had to think and work in natural cycles.

Then one evening after one of Ray's public talks, he was approached by Dr. Dayna Baumeister, a scientist who told him about a new way of working with nature and its cycles – in fact all its rules – and how to do well by doing good. She told him about a process that would soon become a touchstone for him and his company. She told him about biomimicry.

In using biomimicry, one must observe the *pas de deaux* between wild organisms and the forces of wind, precipitation, altitude, and so on – that dance with them. The steps are crucial – because to miss one is to fall out of sync which then requires a restart or recalibration. So it is with nature and those ever-present operating conditions: sunlight, water, gravity, limits and boundaries, dynamic nonequilibrium, and cyclic processes. These define wildness at the most basic level.

Most of us understand the importance of the first three operating conditions, whether we optimize their presence in our daily work and world or not. The fourth, limits and boundaries, is again rather poorly understood. Humans regularly, sometimes proudly and flagrantly, violate limits and boundaries with little respect for how such actions might affect other organisms, including humans, or the planet as a whole.

As to the fifth operating condition, dynamic nonequilibrium, you read how many forces act on any given object in a number of ways to produce the "rolling-ball-in-a-bowl" effect earlier. However, the eminent ecologist C. S. Holling[5] goes further by referring to it as an orange that experiences increasing amounts of third-party pressure (whether from a biological or nonbiological source) until the fruit is suddenly released to shoot forward powerfully rolling higgledy-piggledy around said bowl. So when change happens, it can happen fast and powerfully.

By understanding and applying the final element of cycles and cyclic processes, humans – including those in industry – can achieve some of the most potentially groundbreaking advances in sustainability. Consider the seasons with their cycles of rest and restoration. Birth, growth, and death with the subsequent birth of the next shiny new generation of fungus, plant, or animal provide another portrait of life cycles. "Waste equals food"[6] has become a key concept for the cyclical, circular economy, and increasing numbers of neighboring businesses are now using each other's waste as fuel for their own companies. But to optimize long-term, whether in making the world turn or a business profit, all of these operating conditions of the wild must not only be considered but understood and embraced.

With these foundational conditions, we can peer into nature to see how each organism optimizes with strategies that either work – or pass from the Earth.

During the fateful meeting between Ray and the young scientist who attended his talk, she suggested Ray's people go beyond their laboratories and conference rooms out into the wild to reconnect

BUSINESS FROM THE WILD – INTERFACE, INC. **41**

with and learn from nature's operating systems – and adopt those strategies of the wild.

A short time later, David was tasked with driving to the airport late at night to pick up that young scientist who had shared her knowledge with Ray. Dayna had been hired to run a biomimicry workshop for a mélange of employees who represented every sector of the company, from the manufacturing floor to the marketing department. Dayna and Janine took turns taking the design, production, marketing, and business office team members out into the semi-wild forests surrounding Interface's west-central Georgia offices. On these excursions, they asked that key biomimicry question: *How would nature…?* For Interface, the question revolved around how to better design a floor. Out in the woods, gazing at the carpet of leaves these team members saw an answer – diversity.

"If you look at anything in nature – leaves, flowers, rocks – it's diversity," David observed.

> There is nothing that is the same. Making things the same and uniform is a human enterprise. So, the fundamental principle that I started thinking about was, how can we make carpet tiles diverse, so that each carpet tile will come out different in color and design?

His voice suddenly tensed as he continued,

> This was the complete opposite of what we'd been designing all my life. We'd been designing with uniformity. Each product would have to conform to the same color, same texture, same everything. We would call it 'quality' but we were going against nature's grain.

The result was waste – waste on the cutting room floor, waste when dye lots didn't match, and waste when customers had to purchase extra stock to replace damaged or stained tiles. To counter such waste, David gave the challenge to Sydney Daniel, and together they hit upon a solution, a nonlinear/directional patterned carpet design soon to be named Entropy™.

Meanwhile, over at the Innovation department, biomimicry was following a different beat through Bill. "When I read the biomimicry book, I learned something different from what other people got about the amazing things that nature does. In nature, you fill a hole nobody else can and that's efficient. That works." Bill's role took him down the path of science and math that would yield a profitable product. David's role was to use biomimicry for design and meet Bill at the end of that path.

Then one day there was a mistake.

> To minimize the amount of labor and down time with David's three-toned yarn diversity idea, I had tufted a large sample on the carpet-making mechanism that lets us test new tufting ideas. But we failed to put the directional arrows on the back of the tile so we could tell which way the true direction was

said Bill with a rueful smile. "Well, we kept laying it out and we weren't sure if we had the right runs or different runs mixed together."

Because this would affect everything from the look of the carpet, to packaging, and ultimately to customer satisfaction, they kept turning the squares, flipping them from one place to another. No one could tell which was the "correct" pattern. The chance for creating the same tile pattern was now about 1 in 8,000. Not only would it be easier to manufacture, it had less off-quality and would be easier to package.

They had successfully engaged in two of the three practices required in biomimicry by both connecting or reconnecting with nature and emulating it. By mimicking the diversity they found, they had successfully emulated the forest floor. That allowed them to start complying with the operating systems of the wild.

"This was a kind of shallow foray into the world of biomimicry – looking at it from an aesthetics standpoint," John acknowledged. "But the more we dug in, the more we started to realize that it's about cycles." The more they applied nature's overarching strategies, the more they created a randomness of pattern that customers praised as comforting.

Not trained as psychologists but in need of broader insights about human well-being, the men started asking audiences who attended their public talks to imagine the place on Earth that made them feel most alive.

John remarked,

> About 95% of the time they would say it was outside where they feel most alive. We don't really know the exact reason, but one of the things we've pinpointed is that humans try to control everything. We want to control color. We expect repeating patterns. We want there to be this "exactness" about our interior space, but it's so different from our valued outdoor space. And this exactness affects us at a psychological level.
>
> When you're outside, everything is random. Your brain isn't working overtime to pick up patterns. You're not trying to find flaws – because you accept that there really are no flaws. There are just these cycles of life around you. The wild can make mistakes but its whole remains flawless.

He admits they never really put their finger on the psychological reasons underlying these preferences, but when they started working with natural models, a rhythm of randomness emerged – a rhythm that worked for the engineer, the mathematician, the designer, and the satisfaction of the customer. Biomimicry worked at the plant and the business office too. Outcomes of their first venture into biomimicry included doubling their existing division's sales between 2002 and 2007.

Reduced waste also emerged as a benefit – from the 4% of standard carpet tiles down to 1.5% for the new products. There was no longer a need to reject mismatched dye batches. Recycling and disposal costs decreased significantly, and customer installation costs related to waste plummeted by 70%. Greatest of all, by avoiding the cost and waste of back-stocking replacement floor tiles, they saved customers $110 for every 100 yards ordered – making this the company's most popular line.

Here enters the third element of biomimicry in addition to connecting to and emulating nature – examining the ethics of human intentions and actions with the understanding that humans are only one among the millions of species on Earth. Humans rely on the plenty provided by the natural world. Yet within this plenty a chasm exists between what we have known and understood and what remains mysterious and sometimes dangerous. In modern Western nations, most humans remain uncomfortable with this perceived split, working to subdue and conquer the wild, making it more understandable and useable and less wild in the process. Over time, many cultures began to view extractive and un-wilding practices as an inalienable right to be utilized at almost any environmental cost.

As John reflected on how changes were able to transform the company from a purely extractive entity into one that focused on reconciliation and reciprocity, he recalled his early university training,

> Every single class I had in engineering started with a 'Given' statement that went like this: Assume that raw materials are abundant and consistent. Now think about that. How human is that – to crazily believe we are somehow going to continue to extract oil from the Earth and make consistent materials around which we build an entire system? What if that's *not* true? What if that's a bad assumption?

These were the questions the team began to ask. Their business had been built on arm's length transactions, a process where suppliers exchanged raw materials for cash. They made carpet and exchanged carpet for customers' cash. Because the average customer used their company's product seven years and then sent it to a landfill, the team was experiencing dissonance. They were aiming for sustainability through biomimicry but engaged in a process that at its roots was unsustainable in the long term – both environmentally and economically. The dissonance also had roots in a simple principle that came from knowledge they attained in seventh-grade science: Earth is a closed system in which matter can't be created or destroyed. So when they created waste or customers were throwing away old carpet, it was still there – in a matted, darkened pile, but still there.

John continued,

> So the ideal would be that we could all realize we are a species in a closed system. Everything that goes through us and every other species is going into our closed system. Then, we could figure out, like nature, how to grow together in that closed system.

Knowing the realities of nature's laws and changing the direction of the charging bull that is business, which has historically aimed for the highest profits in the shortest amount of time, has been a matter of patience and vision.

> As a society, we've got this insatiable appetite for more stuff – and it's all disposable. But what if I went to my customers and my colleagues in my supply chain and developed a carpet leasing program? You can give those raw petroleum-based materials back to us and we can build our company more around the labor-heavy business of recycling than the raw materials-heavy business of creating virgin products year after year. It doesn't matter if a guy cares or doesn't care about sustainability… this isn't a belief thing… this is a straight-up numbers thing.

Short-term needs as a CEO of a company, many times responding to a board of directors, beget the tendency to think short-term. A tightrope made of cost reductions pulling on one end and increasing income pulling on the other keeps the rope taut and the CEO aloft. Such an atmosphere begets the language of maximization. Nature's language is optimization. It uses only what it needs to build life. Interface had begun learning the language of optimization. They had Ray's vision of reconciling with nature as a means to do well *and good* in business to guide them as a North Star.

> A lot of times leaders and managers want to eliminate all of the reasons that something will fail before they decide to get behind it. What this does is tell all the people in the project that you don't believe in them. And Ray, John said, leaning in and dropping his voice, "would look for the light at the end of the tunnel, and when he saw it he'd put his arm around you and say – *I'm bettin' on you, Sport.*" "That gives you a focus like no other focus," John nodded. If you think your boss is that guy who's so afraid to step forward, and so reluctant to believe in the human spirit that you don't take on the burden of success, then it's not yours. And if it's not yours, then you're just working for the man. And if you're just working for the man, it's just a job. And if it's just a job, then every other job is just a job, and what investment do you have in it? Ray got that. He got it down to his core.

The team didn't know when they walked out into the woods that the operating conditions discovered there would inspire their most profitable, fastest growing line of carpets. But with Ray as a leader, and a team of people that respected others for their roles on that team, Interface made biomimicry a flagship tool for reconciling with the wild and the operating conditions that drive it.

The team at Interface continues to work with nature's genius through biomimicry, bio-inspiration, and bio-utilization, for example, integrating algae on a carpet background (since algae grow best on a 3D substrate). The patented product is intended to filter and clean water at a variety of landscapes scales, from the Chesapeake Bay to an Arkansas hog farm.

They're also working in multiple ways to recycle carpet, breaking the extractive cycle, putting more people to work, and expanding the program to enrich communities around the world.

The essence of reconciling business with the wild or semi-wild can be found in the ongoing work to respect the roles of nature, its cycles, and needs, which also include our own. Instead of treating ourselves as a species apart, a community that need not heed Earth's Operating Conditions, we can learn, as did Ray and his team, to braid our lives into nature – reconnecting to the continent as part of the main.

INTERFACE LESSONS LEARNED

The central room at Pond Studios, David Oakey's design space, is floor to ceiling windows which make the central Georgia woods – pines, oaks, and variety of wildlife feel like part of the office. The building is modern by design but blends into the woods around it with a buffer zone of gardens filled with native plants. Inside, the central office space is filled with tables covered with boards replete with pictures of client office interiors, fabric swatches, color charts, and samples. There's a big touchy-feely table with all kinds of natural objects in the center – a snake skin, bleached out coral, a turtle shell, antlers, moss – and a diminutive woman next to it all with a kind face and gracious manners.

Sydney Daniel, the graphic designer who originated the design for Interface's Entropy™ carpets, began by telling me the story of

BUSINESS FROM THE WILD – INTERFACE, INC. **47**

when Dayna first came to the studio. Dayna took the group outside to look at nature's carpet which was not uniform. Leaves are not uniform. Pine needles are not uniform. Diversity was the reality they saw surrounding them.

Sydney started working on creating a pattern. They chose the colors and began putting them into simulations. She said it seemed scary at first. They wondered if it was going to be too complicated for manufacturing to handle, but as the project took shape they started to think – why haven't we done this before? Nature isn't about perfect colors or shapes. Why should we try to be? Sydney summed up their thoughts, "Nothing comes to mind that didn't work. *The more like nature, the better it worked.*"

In embarking into this new methodology of biomimicry, it was important that they all learn what biomimicry is, but they also had to be aware of what it isn't. You now know it isn't bio-utilization or biophilia or any of the other cousins. There don't have to be impractical physical or economic requirements to use natural materials. You can emulate materials with other life-friendly substances or recycled materials. One doesn't need to change the larger industrial universe within which one's company exists unless the people in your company think it needs changing.

However, one does need to let go of mythologies which are simply that – mythologies – and take the leap into a new way of working. The Interface family thought their customers both wanted and, in fact, demanded uniformity in their carpets. What they found out was customers valued the nonpatterned patterns nature brought to the end product over uniformity. Interface took a chance on mimicking those varied patterns of the forest floor. That diversity created a new, higher value in reduced material use and cost as well as cost to the environment. At the writing of this book, Oakey Designs is using biomimicry in 60–70% of their work. The randomization of pattern also increased life span because it hid wear and tear. Entropy™ was released in 2000 but is still one of their top five sellers.[7]

This change in methodology also led them to diversify and expand their markets. Along with diversity in design, Interface expanded its consumer market from corporations into schools, government, and health care, among others.[7] Although Entropy™ was the first

48 BUSINESS FROM THE WILD – INTERFACE, INC.

biomimetic offspring of Interface, its success gave rise to i2®, a carpet with light and dark color variation and design elements ideal for those government and large business settings. It is also one of a new corral of flooring products in the Cool Carpet™ program. This program takes corporate sustainability a step further by analyzing and offsetting greenhouse gas emissions in partnership with the Climate Neutral Network and like-minded companies such as Nike and FedEx and even start-ups such as Genomatica sustainable chemicals.

As a starting point though, they began simply. They deployed the basics of biomimicry by mimicking structural aesthetics. As they practiced and stuck with it though, they began looking at cycles more and more and knew that's where they needed to go.

The team started using and wasting less by utilizing recycled yarn, which helped them substantially reduce material use. Reuse creates greater savings while forming a cyclical process, which they had already observed in nature and concluded it was right for business. Then they began looking at alternative sourcing. They reached out to nontraditional partners in the South Pacific to collect used and discarded fishing line for product creation – again, reducing costs and honoring cycles, but now producing jobs as well.

According to David Oakey,

> The whole first year was about doing less damage to the Earth. It's like buying a car that gets more miles to the gallon. You're still driving, still using fossil fuel – but that was our first step. Then we started thinking about redesign and that's where this biomimicry came in – and those principles of nature were a guide.

In fact, when they weren't mimicking nature's patterns and principles, they ended up creating more waste. Instead, the company moved from the 3–4% waste typical in modular carpeting and 14% in roll carpets down to 1.5% – by mimicking the nonpatterned pattern of the forest floor.

But reducing waste wasn't the only place where the company began saving money and reconstructing a healthier relationship with the Earth. Understanding everything can be reclaimed, reused, or recycled led to breakthroughs in recycling – but also water conservation, from two gallons per square yard in 1996 to less than a

BUSINESS FROM THE WILD – INTERFACE, INC. **49**

half-gallon in 2015. *They now also recognize, embrace, and profit from the fact that nature runs off solar income.* Knowing this, they moved to renewable energy and persisted in increasing energy efficiency.[7]

Because of the time lag in the cycle between inception and roll-out of a product and the fact they want biomimicry to be part of the day-to-day; *they began biomimicry training programs inside the company to keep its inspiration and processes in the forefront.* They learned more from Life's Principles as they continued. People from other regions tended to come to the area for a job, but would then leave. *By being locally attuned and hiring local talent, they reduced employee turnover.*

And it's not just biomimicry. In fact, John underscored the importance of biophilia as he noted the relaxation people feel when they're outside *not* trying to identify patterns. As it turns out, people enjoy the random nature of nature. In the case of a carpeting company, that's good for profits and the planet.

ACKNOWLEDGMENTS

In addition to listed references, this chapter is based on interviews conducted in September of 2014 with Interface staff John Bradford, Bill Jones, and Erin Meezan, and both David Oakey and Sydney Daniel of Oakey Designs. I extend my heartiest thanks to them without whom this chapter would not exist. I am also grateful for the visionary leadership and kindness of Mr. Ray Anderson who I had the great pleasure of meeting and working with for too short a time. He embodied reciprocity not only to other humans but to all species. –*MF*

REFERENCES

1 Claus, Anja. "A Language to Embody Place: Dynamic, Braided, Wild." *Minding Nature* 7, No. 3 (2014), 45–46.

2 Biomimicry 3.8. https://Biomimicry.net. Accessed 7 March, 2018.

3 Hawken, Paul. *The Ecology of Commerce.* New York, NY: Harper Collins Publishers, 1993.

4 Quinn, Daniel. *Ishmael an Adventure of the Mind and Spirit.* New York, NY: Bantam Books, 1992.

5 Holling, C. S., and S. Sanderson. *Rights to Nature: Ecological, Economic, Cultural and Political Principles of Institutions for the Environment.* Washington, DC: Island Press, 1996.

6 McDonough, W., and M. Braungart. *Cradle to Cradle.* New York, NY: North Point Press, 2002.

7 Chirazi, J. *Biomimicry Business Intelligence – Financial & Market Research; Biomimicry Business Case Study: Interface.* Biomimicry Advisory Services, 2015.

SPIRALING INTO SUCCESS – PAX SCIENTIFIC

A worn path may or may not yield success,
but a new path invites it.

Squinting his eyes as he studied the sparkling water, Jay watched his hands pull whirlpools alongside the wooden dinghy as he rolled with the Australian surf. How could a nine-year-old have guessed those liquid funneled shapes would lead him to start future multi-million-dollar businesses and be called upon to lecture audiences all around the world? At that age he just knew the ocean was more appealing than the classroom – or anywhere else.

Bronzing sun shone down as he fashioned a little spear to catch fish. Patiently, patiently he waited and watched as his shining quarry veered left and right reflecting silver, shooting past him. Over time he began to observe fish shapes. They were so much better suited to water life than he was. Their torpedo outlines created a streamlined path of least resistance. And the seaweed they swam through, while fragile enough to snap in his hands, could withstand the most violent of storms and powerful waves. Watching the plants spin with the tides, he began to notice a common geometry of motion they followed. Although constantly moving and changing, the leaves were formed so as to relieve the pressure of the waves – again following the path of least resistance.

Back in school his teachers sighed. Labeled as lazy, Jay Harman couldn't process what teachers were trying to instill – not when there were so many things to think about outside school walls. Many days found him staring out the window with his teachers constantly trying to redirect him. His mind, however, was offshore with those shining torpedoes, swaying branches, and the archetypal shapes that created – motion.

Eventually, and with the encouragement of his mother, Jay attended college to study electrical engineering. Wrapped in the confines of academia, Jay was miserable. Finally after two tortuous years, he left to work at the Department of Fisheries and Wildlife as a naturalist and boat captain. During his time there, Jay was also appointed as a county supervisor. Hoping to protect special wild places in his home town, he instead saw again and again those special areas subjected to the bulldozer's indiscriminate blade. Although he was vocal, he was often unable to stop the destruction. Reflecting on it, Jay observed there was no way to protect nature long-term unless human aspirations were satisfied. He had to take that knowledge and figure out how to work with it to make a difference for nature, while somehow making a living.

Even though he left school, he had been attending "university" his whole life – from the seat of a dinghy to a little while in an actual classroom and now in a patrol boat – still learning about nature. How do fish move? How does seaweed move? How do fluids move? How does nature move? How would built objects like boats behave when subjected to nature's forces of motion? These were his fascination points as a child and, it turned out, as a man. So it seemed natural this would figure into his next steps at work.

When asked about his life then and how he began working to mimic nature, Jay reflects,

> I think really – creativity comes from being immersed in something you're fascinated by – you know, as they say, follow your passion. If you're fascinated, you troll for additional knowledge and you learn. Sometimes you learn because people are teaching you and sometimes you find your own particular way because you're just fascinated. All that adds up to creativity.

Jay was fascinated by nature and the movement within nature.

> We all like to look at campfires, at lightning, at waves on a beach. What we're looking at is movement, with all its archetypal shapes – the moment to moment changes in shape and positioning based on the flow of water or air – the forces around whatever you're watching.

All he could see was movement. The solid world disappeared as he studied the swirling bits of energy within movement. He realized movement itself was at the core of everything.

Jay continued trolling for ideas and lessons in nature and found particular shapes were common to all movement he studied. He realized every living thing is built according to certain geometries and that the efficiencies nature produced were superior to those of human designs.

So Jay did what many people do. He started a business based around his passion. It was a company based on something he knew was needed, an energy research group focusing on the efficiencies he had found in those natural geometries. But he did so without performing sufficient market testing first. At the end of the day, he found that, because energy was cheap, nobody cared. They might have "needed" it, but they didn't "want" it at the time. What he needed was something a little less radical – and a little more *wild*.

Jay saw that modern boat designs were lacking in many ways. Motor boats had dangerous propellers. They had storage and maintenance issues, and were expensive compared to other recreational vehicles so were owned by fewer people. Jay intended to address all those issues and hopefully get more people out on the water with the invention of a boat he called the Wild Thing.

Along with building small fishing spears as a boy, Jay had also built various small boats. Over the years, not only had Jay become a captain of patrol and research craft, he had also built his own sailboat on which he logged nearly 30,000 miles.

More recently, Jay made boats with see-through bottoms for children he was mentoring. A number of the children feared the ocean and therefore the snorkeling trips he put together for the group. To help them experience the same undersea world his other kids were seeing through masks, Jay developed a transparent boat out of industrial plastic. This allowed the kids to join in the exploration and watch life in the ocean unfold below them.

When the kids weren't roving in the boat, Jay would get in and lie on the bottom, watching how the water interacted with the shape and material of the craft. There at water level, he was reintroduced to the shapes he had seen in nature over the years. He recalled both the swirling whirlpools and how swans and ducks didn't leave much of a bow wave as they swam with effortless ease.

54 SPIRALING INTO SUCCESS – PAX SCIENTIFIC

At night when the children were sleeping, he sat down and wrote a list.

- What features would a really optimized boat have?
- What problems would it solve?
- What are the attributes of an ideal boat?

Even though he wasn't asking how nature would do it he had been immersed in nature so long, he found himself adapting what he had already learned from the fish and the kelp and the ducks. When asked about that, he demurs,

> The nature of invention is such that it usually doesn't come from the author. It comes from someplace else. It's given to us. Masters of history reveal this with many innovators. Radical innovation comes from flashes of inspiration – even between the thoughts we usually have. It's not as much one plus one equals two. It's as much about feeling my way through the design as anything – because I've observed nature for so long.

After completing his list, Jay taped up sheets of old white wrapping paper the length of one wall in his house and five feet high. He reflected on his questions and how he knew nature would accomplish those goals, "feeling" his way into designing the Wild Thing – his first commercial success in the boat business.

Jay believed, and still does, that when you are building a business – whether you need a manufacturer, a marketer, a materials person, or an engineer – you get the best that exists. Even if you can't afford to build the product, at least you have gotten the domain expert to tell you how to build the product and make sure it's buildable. You also need to make sure they can operate in the language of the day, so when you get done, you've got a plan anyone can understand. Here's the concept. Here's why it will work. Here are the people who can make it, and here's what it will cost. One. Two. Three. Four.

So, of course, when he rolled up those papers and stuffed them in his satchel, the person's office he was taking them to was naturally a domain expert – a designer of winning America's Cup yachts – in fact, one of the world's leading naval architects.

SPIRALING INTO SUCCESS – PAX SCIENTIFIC **55**

Jay told him his understanding of movement and fluid dynamics and how he wanted to mimic the geometries used by living organisms. He rolled it out on the table before the man, and the man said,

It won't work. That's not how you build a boat.

But Jay wanted the man to enter the plans into his computer so he could get some proper CAD blueprints.

"Well, could you humor me?" Jay asked.
"I'd be wasting your money."
"I'd still like you to do it."

So, the Naval architect went away to work on it, but when he came back to Jay, he had drawn a conventional boat design.

"This not what I paid you for. Would you please go back and do what I asked you?"
"Well, if it works I'll eat my hat," the designer said.
"Bring your knife and fork."

The designer finally acquiesced, and when they launched the boat and it worked, the designer was shocked – which Jay quite enjoyed.

Jay, however, was already looking forward to his next move. In order to avoid working with "heavy, nasty fiberglass," Jay planned to thermoform his boats with the transparent, industrial plastic he had used for the smaller boats. That would mean he could build the basic boat in four minutes with virtually no labor.

Knowing the process was going to require a lot of capital with the materials, full-size molds for prototypes, and molding machines to carry it all off, Jay headed to Outboard Marine Corporation (OMC), north of Chicago. At the time, OMC was a giant in the marine world. Though he's still not sure how he, "a little hayseed from western Australia," managed it, he made a presentation to their board of directors. He entered the high-gloss board room and presented his small boat prototype along with his summation on the niche it could fill in the boat industry.

Referring back to his experience with children, Jay closed the deal by saying,

You guys make all your money on big engines but you're losing market share to others. If you start out with small engines and boats for children, you can use this smaller boat as a loss leader and build brand loyalty like the auto companies do, for when your customers become adults. You guys have first crack at this but if you pass, I'm driving up the road to your largest competitor and offering it to them.

Not wanting that the directors took an exclusive option, wrote Jay a check large enough for a full-sized mold and several boats. When he returned to show off these boats modeled after nature's geometries and fluid dynamics, he garnered an order for 5,000 units. Modeling nature in his process meant Jay's boats were cheaper to build and operated on a third less energy. It was hailed as the most successful and efficient small boat design in the world.

The success of the Wild Thing craft occurred in 1990. By 1997, the same year Janine wrote her book, he was ready to use the process on a new company. When he began in business, the man had to borrow $20 to buy a white shirt for a presentation of his ideas. By the time he was ready to start PAX Scientific, he had already put his first highly successful technology company (the one people weren't ready for at the time) on the stock market. He applied the proceeds from that success to further advances in biomimicry. By immersing himself in nature and earnestly observing the interactions between fluids and organisms, Jay had been practicing biomimicry before the modern biomimicry movement had even begun. He persisted, and he was finally and certainly operating at a profit.

On his journey Jay found the shape of a particular spiral again and again in nature – in calla lilies and seashells, cactus and swirling clouds, the fiddlehead of a fern, and vortices in water. Starting at such a young age, Jay accepted the efficiency of nature's spirals as a simple fact in his world view. Without analyzing it, he came to understand nature repeats itself in many materials and processes when it finds something that works – and the spiral he found from calla lilies to vortices worked well at moving water and air efficiently.

This ended up being fortuitous as modern municipalities have a host of challenges with water treatment plants. Costs of moving water from rivers, lakes, and groundwater through water treatment plants and on to our houses, efficiencies required in filters, and, of course, laying endless miles of pipe all figure prominently into their costs and their customers' bills. However, one of the most perplexing problems revolves around the storage of processed water.

When chlorinated water is stored over a period of time, the products used to disinfect the water age. As they do, particularly in warmer weather, their effectiveness can decline. They can also begin to stratify into layers of warmer, older water which can create by-products unhealthy for the people drinking them. Water officials are constantly on the watch for not only these by-products but the conditions under which they are formed.

Knowing this and armed with the knowledge of how nature's spirals have the capacity to efficiently move large amounts of water, Jay began work on something he eventually patented as the "lily impeller." Only six inches tall and able to move 10 million gallons of water, the impeller reduces energy use to the equivalent of three 100-watt lightbulbs as well as decreasing the mixing time and a number of by-products arising from the stored water. It also reduces capital costs and helps prevent nitrification and potential damage from ice.

"I'm sure you're familiar with my little water mixer," Jay beams like a proud Papa.

> It's 100% effective in 100% of the applications. It's a tiny little thing and when I took it out to engineers, municipalities and manufacturers at first, they were insulting. People ridiculed me and trying to get financial backing was extremely difficult. Basically the people who funded my efforts in the early days were a poet and a number of people who loved nature and saw that there was beauty in what I was trying to do.

Over 20 years, Jay found there was no substitute for the grind. Time and time again, Jay promoted his inventions and eventually they began to be tested. The government validated them. Universities validated them. Municipalities of all sizes began using the mixer emulating the lily, nautilus shells, and those vortices of water Jay pulled past his boat as a boy. They are now used in thousands of tanks from Manitoba and Missouri to the Middle East.

PAX Scientific has created a number of subsidiaries, including PAX Mixer, PAX Air, PAX Pure, and PAX Water Technologies. Involved now in everything from refrigeration fans to water desalinization; with its 25% more efficient refrigeration fans alone, PAX is effectively tackling a subset of energy use in the U.S. that represents 22% of our total energy consumed.

Today Jay has a flotilla of employees drawn in by the success of his companies — but also for the thought processes behind them. While Jay is spending more and more time bringing attention to how the world views and deals with fluid dynamics, he leaves his employees with this,

> What I tell my folks is what I see as the only commandment — only do that which creates the conditions for life. Whether considering toxic chemicals or fan blades; ask how can you use the least material with the least energy? If you're truly biomimetic you're leaving no waste.

PAX SCIENTIFIC LESSONS LEARNED

Jay has been a biomimeticist-in-training since he was a boy. Those interactions with nature at nine and ten that sprang out of simple curiosity ultimately led him to success in business. Later as a designer and entrepreneur, he saw biomimicry as a logical and useful methodology. As he deployed it to solve one problem, he found he had the forms and structures to solve another — spawning more growth in his companies as new inventions became realities. He came to biomimicry as a way to build a business and continued it to help avert environmental disasters he saw looming. Today Jay works to be restorative — reducing waste, energy, and material usage while developing further benefits to his customers. He uses a combination of biophilia, bio-inspiration, and biomimicry. He also mimics nature's physical forces which are governed, like those life forces, by Earth's operating systems. Here's a little of what he's learned on his journey.

Creativity and fascination with nature can develop a starting block for innovation in business. Lifelong interests in nature can unfurl solution pathways, which can then help solve a problem or build a successful career utilizing nature's genius. (This also begs the question as to why we aren't making sure our children spend more time outside, but that's another book.) Asking questions born out of a desire to see how we might fit elegantly and productively alongside other organisms and the elemental forces of wind, rain, temperature, and so on can yield new ways of problem-solving.

In this creative process, flashes of inspiration are critical to acknowledge and nurture along the way. This doesn't mean endlessly daydreaming without application. Nurturing creativity is not an all or nothing proposition nor does it need to take up endless work hours. What it does mean is that we need to make a space for moving beyond the traditional into a space fertile for inspiration. Time outside can support us in these efforts – time spent observing how nature carries out endless functions – in fact, many of the same functions we're trying to accomplish: creating strength without additional weight, keeping moisture off, encouraging moisture to stay, protecting materials during transport, and so many others. Instead of constantly following the same rote processes in the same way day after day, moving outside as part of one's problem-solving process can open up a space for crucial inspiration.

As Jay models nature's shapes, he has found he can work with a number of materials and consistently end up with products requiring up to a third less energy and structures that can be utilized for a number of purposes. As we've read in other company stories, it is easy (and perhaps a general first step) to look only at shape when working in biomimicry. However, those same innovators, like Jay, also urge new practitioners to go deeper. *Observe natural processes. Consider mimicking natural or benign materials. Examine systems.* In these ways, we can move beyond just sticking a widget onto a machine to perform a function.

We might, to better effect, take into account the entire context of the problem and create a higher functioning and much more elegant solution. Additionally, if we choose optimization over maximization and examine, then utilize cycles of both energy and materials along with mimicking processes and systems; financial savings can be multiplied and by-products can be functional while contributing to community health and environmental well-being. Beyond the benefits connected to the original function being solved for, *biomimicry can produce a ripple effect of benefits.* The lily impeller works to mix water in storage tanks to reduce potentially harmful by-products, but also

60 SPIRALING INTO SUCCESS – PAX SCIENTIFIC

helps prevent water stored in tanks from freezing and damaging equipment. These secondary and even tertiary benefits of the lily impeller include cost savings in maintenance. From 2007 to at least 2015, when these interviews took place, PAX Water has not been required to replace a single impeller due to breakdown.[1]

But biomimicry doesn't exist in a vacuum within the solution-activation arms of companies. Research and development (R&D) plays a critical role in innovation and costs real money. Because this company started out as a biomimetic company, it reinvests 30% of profits back into R&D[1] – the dance partner who brought them here in the first place. They have, of course, also recognized the importance of and secured their inventions with vital patent protections.[1] *PAX has enhanced long-term gains retaining lessons learned by conducting research, design, and much of the testing internally.* However, they do contract out the building of their products.[1] *Also, because they chose ways to develop products to support larger partner companies around them, they've profited from the marketing programs and reach of those same companies as well as selling and distributing to their networks.*[1]

And they are still hiring domain experts here and in all aspects of their work in areas where the team has little expertise. They reward them for their expertise and enjoy the results. *But first, they ensure these experts can communicate by learning the language of biom* and PAX's particular dialect of the methodology.* Even within the company, although engineers and designers don't always speak the same language, at PAX they are brought to a team because of their willingness and ability to communicate.[1]

Here, as in any new company or company marketing new products, it has been critical for their team to refrain from underestimating time to market and/or time for market penetration.[1] Consumers have to be ready for innovation and that innovation must fill a need. Just because efficiency was a good idea when Jay first started, didn't mean it was marketable. Because energy was cheap when he founded his first company, few people listened. Today few people ignore him, but he and his company take special pains to analyze and predict timing. For example, the company utilized extensive market research and Beta testing over a year allowing PAX to educate potential customers and prove the value of their mixers. *These days they also work to address existing markets (customers) but also seek out new ones as Jay did when exploring market development in youth boats to build brand loyalty.*[1] Within the company, they have retained loyalty by offering inside investment through employees and stakeholders.[1]

At the time of this writing, the company continues to celebrate 40% growth per year. *Still, there is no substitute for the grind.*

ACKNOWLEDGMENTS

This chapter is based on an interview conducted in February 2015 with Jay Harman. I thank Jay for sharing his time, descriptions of his life, and his vision for a world doing better by learning from nature. −*MF*

REFERENCE

1 Chirazi, J. *Biomimicry Business Intelligence − Financial & Market Research; Biomimicry Business Case Study: PAX Water Technologies.* Biomimicry Advisory Services, 2015.

NURSE SHARKS IN YOUR HOSPITAL – SHARKLET TECHNOLOGIES, INC.

> The ocean looks beautiful from a distance.
> The gathering and release of each wave against the shore creates lullabies
> when you're not right there confronted with it – confronted with failure again, again.
> And yet you persist.
> And one morning, a pearl.

It stank of sea urchins stranded at high tide – rotting. Salty beads of perspiration adhered to sunburned skin as Tony stared at his panels, surrounded by seawater and covered with barnacles, tube worms, and green tresses of algae.

"It's too bad we're not getting paid to make things stick to those panels," one of the scientists joked with an acerbic edge. Kidding – not kidding.

Four managers from the Office of Naval Research stood in the shade of the massive dock conferring, their crisp button-down shirts reflecting too much light.

Pearl Harbor is always busy – bustling with reverent tourists, military personnel, university students, scientists, and on this day a building-sized nuclear submarine heading out of port. From their position on the raft below the looming dock, they could still see the slightly crusted waterline on the sub's conning tower curving up at both ends like a meniscus in a test tube separating the usually dry upper tower from the metal generally resting below sea level where slippery algae clung.

Dr. Anthony Brennan, a venerable materials science and engineering professor from the University of Florida, had been partnering with a team from England to discover how to keep swimming plant cells, barnacles, tube worms, and any other organisms that tried from affixing themselves to the hulls of naval ships. Not just a matter of spit and polish, these organisms increased drag on ships costing the Navy around $56 million in fuel and maintenance costs.[1] Beyond that fact, the increased drag inhibited acceleration to the point they sometimes couldn't get up to speed to launch jets. In effect, some ships were transformed into really expensive helicopter bases.

Up until Tony teamed with James and Maureen Callow at the University of Birmingham in England, the Navy had only one way to deal with the little buggers. Every five years or so, they pulled the ship up out of its ocean home to scrub, scrape, and repaint everything below the waterline – generally with a copper-based paint or something equally as objectionable for its effects on living organisms in the proximity of the ship. With the cost of that potential harm, the actual dollars spent, and the time spent keeping ships out of commission during the process, the Navy was determined to find another way of doing business.

Tony and the team had started their work together on this fractious problem by examining how Ulva linza zoospores (basically swimming plant cells) attached to ship hulls and how other scientists were attempting to solve the problem. Textures like sandpaper, screens, and other rough surfaces had been tried and found wanting. The challenge was to find a surface that inhibited organisms from settling there. So, Tony shifted away from grainy textures to constructing tiny pillars – on the order of two microns tall and two microns apart – really tiny. These were the panels he sent to Pearl Harbor for testing.

He squinted as he watched the sub. Feeling more than a little deflated and even more annoyed, he fumed, "It looks like a big whale." And then, almost as much to himself as to the others, Tony murmured, "You know, whales are heavily fouled. They've got barnacles and sponges and everything all over them."

Suddenly everyone was talking.

"You know, it's a mammal, but dolphins and porpoises are mammals and they stay clean …"

"But they're always moving …"

64 SHARKLET TECHNOLOGIES, INC.

Tony's mind was racing. No on manatees. No on sea turtles. Both get highly fouled. What moves slowly and doesn't get fouled?

"Sharks!"

The group kept talking, "No they're always moving...."

But Tony was lost in thought. He remembered seeing sedentary nurse sharks at aquariums. These sharks had the ability to be still, sometimes even resting on their fins on the ocean floor. Even when active, these sharks could hover in low-velocity currents – much like those experienced by ships when docked. That's when most organisms attached – but they didn't with sharks. Why?

As soon as he worked this out in his head, Tony turned to Geoff Swain, a research colleague at the Florida Institute of Technology.

"Sure, I can catch a shark and we can look at its skin."

"Yes well, we don't want to hurt it, but I can send you a dental impression kit." Tony had formerly worked in dental ceramics for Coors Biomedical in Colorado. "Just take an impression of the skin. It won't hurt the shark. It'll take 30 seconds – and then send it to me."

Geoff was true to his word, and within a couple of weeks Tony was peering at shark skin under an optical profilometer examining the texture of the shark's hide in 3D. As he looked at the dental stone model of the impression, Tony recognized the similarities between the shark's skin and the sample he had been constructing.

He checked in with the university's Museum of Natural History to examine more skin samples. They revealed a pattern comprised of scalelike formations. Although they were attached to the skin, from the side they looked rather like a mushroom with a base, a stem, and a cap. Only the cap was exposed with a rough diamond shape comprised of a series of ridges. From the top, it looked much like a hand on a tabletop with fingers spread slightly apart. A long central ridge was bordered by two shorter ridges on either side and two shorter ones on the outside of those. Voila! A diamond shape appeared.

Tony drew this up and developed a mathematical model with the diamonds side by side. The result was a wave pattern he could then apply to the panel. He called it "Sharklet."

Although he still didn't know exactly what he had besides a mathematical model, Tony was still thinking of that sedentary shark with no fouling. It was time to test the surface on the larger multicellular animals actually plaguing the Navy – barnacles and tube worms. However, tube worms require a colony of bacteria on which to grow. A colleague specializing in these bacteria (*Cobetia marina*) tried repeatedly to grow the bacteria on new panels with no luck.

That's when Tony reexamined the panels and saw that the bacteria were very limited on the surfaces where the pillars were. Although the Hawaiian team had thought they were simply having problems with the test, Tony wondered if it might be something more. As luck would have it, a student from the chemical engineering department heard about the Sharklet work and dropped by Tony's office to see if he could work with him.

"What have you been doing in your own lab work?" Tony queried.

"We were culturing E. coli from a water treatment facility," the student answered.

"Well, then yes, take this film sample down to the lab and grow some of those bacteria on it."

The quite delighted student left, sample in hand. But in a couple of days he returned crestfallen, unable to grow the bacteria. Back and forth he went again and again. Tony sent other grad students to help. He sent the student to other microbiology professors for help. The fact was that the guy was doing everything right. Not only that, life operates in such a way that every species has the tools to ensure their kind survives. In the case of bacteria, they create billions of bacterial cells precisely so their species continues. And yet, no growth. Finally, Tony just told him to write up what he had and he'd take a look.

A few days passed before the always busy professor was able to examine the results. Finally, he projected them up onto the institutional tan wall of his office. While chatting with a colleague, he mildly viewed the slides when all of a sudden it dawned on him, "I told the poor kid to grow E. coli! The reason he was failing wasn't

66   SHARKLET TECHNOLOGIES, INC.

because of anything he was doing. It was because *it wouldn't grow on the surface!"*

The projected image clearly showed – *Escherichia coli* bacteria wouldn't culture on the Sharklet.

Tony then went back into the lab himself comparing bacterial growth (or lack of it) on Sharklet to its growth on other surfaces. Bacteria, or any organism for that matter, live in a thrifty manner conserving as much energy as possible. You'll remember this as one of life's principles – less energy used, less fuel needed. Optimization is key. It's why a cheetah hunts in such a way that it expends a terrific burst of energy for a carefully considered kill, and then lounges for hours on end – not laziness – conservation of energy. Bacteria behave in the same way cheetahs do; only their quest has to do with finding a suitable surface on which to attach. In sample after sample, bacteria were busily attaching to other surfaces, while time after time on the Sharklet they simply ran out of steam and died. And it wasn't that the Sharklet was killing them. It simply wasn't letting them attach.

As the results became more routine, Tony knew it was time to apply for his patent. A matter of course for university researchers, Tony already held over 40 patents for a university famously known for developing very lucrative products, like Gatorade. Although Tony was still more interested in improving the 85% reduction in algae growth and the 97% reduction in barnacle growth he had attained for the Navy, who had been very supportive, he was being urged by the university to consider Sharklet as a business.

That's when a visit from a personal friend turned professional.

Greg Garvis was originally hired by Tony as a technician back at Coors Biomedical 20 years prior. Greg left Coors to build start-ups, which he later sold at hefty profits. The two had remained friends though, and on this visit when Greg asked Tony what he was up to, Tony described a recent Discovery Channel segment on his process of mimicking shark skin to yield a bacteria-resistant surface. Greg lasered in and immediately asked if he could bring some business colleagues to discuss the material further with Tony as a possible business venture.

> You can't talk to me. You've got to go to the university and talk to them.

Greg spoke with the university and was back the next week with a Certified Public Accountant friend, Dan Seff, and a colleague of his, Joe Bagan. Joe, a former cable executive, was looking for a new business start-up opportunity as well. When the four met for dinner at Tony's home, a business plan was drawn up napkin-style with Joe following up by negotiating a licensing deal with the university.

Pooling resources, initial funding was secured and one of Joe's former mentees at Adelphia Communications, Mark Speicker, joined the group as Chief Operating Officer. Joe agreed to be Chief Executive Officer and Tony became Chief Technical Officer. By January 2008, Sharklet was more than a material; it was a business.

Tony had been clear at the start-up meeting and later in business meetings, "First and foremost, we can never do any harm. We must make things better. If we do any harm we must remove it immediately. We will not endanger anybody or the environment."

All the partners were in agreement and at that point, Tony moved beyond marine species and started more testing of Sharklet on disease-causing bacteria like *E. coli* and *Staph.*[1] The results were the same. No bacteria could grow on the surfaces. But instead of killing them like traditional antibacterial treatments that poison or puncture, Sharklet simply "shed" them by not allowing them to attach. Because of its waves of micro-pillars, bacteria couldn't lodge themselves effectively and multiply. A further benefit of this "shedding" was that unlike traditional approaches with Sharklet, chemicals, including heavy metals, were not present to leach out into or onto the surrounding environment. This meant if Sharklet were to be applied in, say, medical settings, it could be both kind to the patient and kind to the environment simultaneously.

Almost 2 million hospital acquired infections occur each year in the U.S. alone, with almost 100,000 people dying as a result. According to the Centers for Disease Control and Prevention, the cost associated with these infections reaches an estimated $20 billion annually. With this information, the target market became clear. So, over the next seven years, the team began work to develop and implement technologies in the biomedical field that would allow them to reproduce Sharklet onto surfaces – surfaces needing to shed bacteria.

---

1 *Staphylococcus aureus* and *S. epidermidis.*

No manufacturing process to accomplish that existed at the time. So, they worked to apply Sharklet to films in order to cover items and create molding processes to integrate it into surface textures. As with many manufacturing processes, the trial and error took time although Tony, Mark, and the others believed if they could stop pathogens like MRSA (Methicillin-resistant Staphylococcus aureus), it would be well worth their travails.

Of course, business development requires capital, and the bio-medical industry is notorious for the high dollars required to cover all the steps resulting from innovations – to make sure treatments are both safe and effective. The team searched for and received roughly $4 million in grants from an array of interested government sources like the National Institutes of Health (NIH), the Small Business Innovation Research program, and the Department of Defense (DOD) which had been an original investor in the idea. Additionally, a little over $5 million was raised from angel investors. They applied for and received their first half dozen patents with many more in the pipeline. Next came clinical trials which Mark knew would require seven to ten years but luckily were possible because of partnerships existing with DOD and the Veterans Administration.

Unfortunately, another challenge came about when they discovered the only tests that existed within the trial regime were those for treatments that would *kill* bacteria. Nothing existed to test treatments that *shed* bacteria. They thought if they could hold out until 2016 or 2017, their first device could actually be deployed and helping people.

> "Get it in people and start saving lives. That's when we'll be able to scale up," Mark nodded earnestly.

The Foley catheter, for urinary issues, was the first device to be tested. By 2011, studies showed bacterial colonies were being almost cut in half, and the area they covered diminished by over 75%.[2] An endotracheal tube followed with a 99% reduction in bacterial attachment on the Sharklet surface compared to smooth ones.[3] Next came a central venous catheter. This device reduced *Staph* bacteria by 65% in only one hour.[4] A wound dressing called, aptly, Sharkskin was then tested and yielded 64% faster wound closures.[5] An extremely promising adhesively backed film was produced. Although it was ancillary to those devices actually applied onto or inside the body, it would still be able to reduce bacteria on surfaces like bed and hallway railings as well as sink vanities and other areas where bacteria collect.

During this time, the group received another NIH research grant for $1.2 million. A licensing agreement was negotiated with Cook Medical to produce the urinary catheter and scale-up production. Sharklet also began generating revenue with over $1 million in sales in 2012. Since then, the team has developed an iPhone case and is working in partnership with companies like LG International, Steelcase, Sappi North America, and others on products like furniture and new paper-molding technology to increase the shedding of bacteria on even more surfaces.

> "I believe the invention of Sharklet itself was a leap, but I think now it's become an incremental development – which is a classic business model. You must prove things every step of the way." Dr. Tony breathed. "Mother Nature's too complex for us to monetize quickly."

Too complex? Perhaps, but a brilliant biological strategy – and with partnerships growing and revenues starting to build – it was a brilliant model on which to build a business saving lives. And on a sandy seafloor off the coast, a nurse shark stirred.

SHARKLET LESSONS LEARNED

Researchers, businessmen, and women are often accused of cold indifference to the environment. Yet throughout this book and in many businesses deploying biomimicry and its cousins, one sees a continuum of care and even reciprocity take place with and toward nature. A continuum of care can be thought of as a horizontal line with an array of triple bottom-line business procedures along its length. Wasting less and utilizing fewer natural resources while providing healthy work environments and similarly healthy products and services as business outcomes and outputs increase in impact and frequency as one moves across the line. Toward the right-hand end of the continuum, practices actually become regenerative in nature. Businesses use their own waste to create new products. They invest in natural resources. Bridgestone Americas, Inc., as one example, has done this to great effect enhancing natural habitats around many of its plants and supporting nonprofit partners also working to protect and conserve natural resources. The further one moves along the line, the more reciprocity one encounters.

In the case of Sharklet, Tony required their company to do no harm. He flatly stated at the outset, "We will not endanger anybody or the environment." Others in this book and out in the world go so far as to target restorative behaviors, processes, and product lines. That's what Ray Anderson did. Both approaches, although located in slightly different places along the reciprocity continuum, can work for business, people, and nature. *They both begin with intention.*

In keeping bacteria or other organisms away, it's not always necessary to kill them. Nature, and now Sharklet Technologies, Inc., can keep organisms away simply by not providing them with what they need to survive. In the case of Sharklet, it's a matter of surface texture. If they can't hang on, they can't hang out. Imagine how different our approach and resulting impacts to the environment and human health could be if we simply denied creatures like mosquitos and fleas what they need for survival. If an organism doesn't have food, water, shelter, and space in the proper arrangement, they'll simply go elsewhere. Period.

Because of this, the leaders of Sharklet have identified additional markets and zones for prospective growth outside hospitals as well. *In fact, wherever we have formerly tried to kill bacteria is a potential new growth zone for the company.* Although they targeted films, original equipment manufacturing, and medical devices in their initial business plan, they have expanded to new devices such as intraocular lenses used in cataract surgeries. The use of Sharklet here can reduce development of secondary cataracts in patients.

Hospital-acquired infections are a critical issue. And if the solution is a texture rather than a chemical, that could inadvertently create a bacterial resistance, *Sharklet not only had a market – they had a niche market.* Of the roughly 2 million people infected in hospitals annually, "…one hundred thousand of them die because of those infections, which cost the industry almost $30 billion a year to treat, litigate, compensate, and correct,"[6] not to mention the human suffering connected to loss of life.

SHARKLET TECHNOLOGIES, INC. **71**

Because of this, patents in biomimicry, as with other disruptive technologies, are considered by many a critical early step in keeping copycats at bay. This clarion call has been echoed by several of the companies mentioned here. History is heavy with names of those who lost fortunes, credit, or both because they didn't apply for patents or did not do so before someone else beat them to it. You are probably familiar with the name Alexander Graham Bell, but do you know Elisha Gray? One of these fellows simply beat the other to the patent office. However patent applications can be turned down, or worse, someone from elsewhere can steal the idea anyway and profit from it. Unless and until the true inventor challenges them in court and wins, they can continue their dishonest practices. But confronting copycats is costly and some choose to bypass this process for that reason or various others connected to establishing markets or simply benevolence.

In the case of Sharklet, patents were completed early in the company's development. Their business model began with an innovation leap, which is common. Then they progressed to the classic incremental business model which moves at more of an inch-by-inch pace. *This is part of why planning ahead for time to market and market saturation can be so critical.*

As they moved forward, multi-sector investments from an array of stakeholders who could benefit from the technology in some form were key. A collaboration with Cook Medical allowed Sharklet to "reduce risk, speed up time to market for the urinary catheter, and avoid diluting equity in the company further by being required to undergo another round of... raising capital from outside investors."[6] Another, with Sappi North America, allowed for the creation of release papers which assisted them in fashioning textured surfaces by transferring textures onto coated fabrics. *Numerous business innovations and designs require the development of fabrication processes for the disruptive innovations discovered. This creates an additional requirement for capital but can also open up these entirely new markets.* A third example was the collaboration with FLEXcon to develop adhesive films and $10\times$ microstructures to electoform the pattern onto surfaces. After these initial forays, the company looked toward creating its own manufacturing capabilities.[6]

In the complex medical business world, time, money, and patience are critical to make it through to the medical trial stages. Branding, marketing, and selling are additional elements requiring time, but persistence and additional capital to bridge this period are vital. As initial funding from grants and angel investors was used up, a quick, workable launch strategy was created with an eye toward profitability. Their plum position as the sole producer in the new field of surface medical bacterial reduction brought Sharklet to the cusp of company viability and indeed primacy. This made them a juicy target for takeover by a larger medical company, and in May 2017, it was announced that Bagan and Spiecker worked with Peaceful Union to transition the firm to new ownership with additional sources of capital where it is flourishing today.

ACKNOWLEDGMENTS

In addition to listed references, this chapter is based on interviews conducted in the winter and spring of 2015 with Dr. Anthony Brennan of the University of Florida and Founder/Chairman of Sharklet Technologies, Inc. as well as Mark Spiecker, Chief Executive Officer of Sharklet Technologies, Inc. I offer my gratitude and deepest thanks to them for their work in biomimicry and their time and wisdom, which helped create this chapter. −MF

REFERENCES

1 Michael, Hart. "Researchers Tackle Barnacles from a Different Perspective". *News Releases from the U.S. Naval Research Laboratory.* January 17, 2017. https://www.nrl.navy.mil/news/releases/researchers-tackle-barnacles-different-perspective Accessed 15 March, 2018.

2 May, Rhea M., Matthew G. Hoffman, Melinda J. Sogo, Albert E. Parker, George A. O'Toole, Anthony B. Brennan, and Shravanthi T. Reddy. "Micro-patterned Surfaces Reduce Bacterial Colonization and Biofilm Formation In Vitro: Potential for Enhancing Endotracheal Tube Designs". *Clinical and Translational Medicine,* 3, No. 8 (2014). doi:10.1186/2001-1326-3-8

3 Reddy, Shravanthi T., Kenneth K. Chung, Clinton J. McDaniel, Rabih O. Darouiche, Jaime Landman, and Anthony B. Brennan. "Micro-patterned Surfaces for Reducing the Risk of Catheter-Associated Urinary Tract Infection: An In Vitro Study on the Effect of Sharklet Micro-patterned Surfaces to Inhibit Bacterial Colonization and Migration of Uropathogenic Escherichia coli". *Journal of Endourology,* 25, No. 9 (2011), 1547–1552. doi:10.1089/end.2010.0611.

4 May, Rhea M., Matthew G. Hoffman, Dipankar Manna, and Shravanthi T. Reddy. *Micro-patterned Polyurethane Surfaces for Reducing Bacterial Attachment Associated with Catheter-Associated Blood Stream Infections.* Aurora, CO: Sharklet Technologies, Inc. National Heart Lung and Blood Institute.

5 Sharklet Technologies Inc. http://sharklet.com/our-products/wound-healing/. Accessed 20 March, 2017.

6 Chirazi, J. *Biomimicry Business Intelligence – Financial & Market Research; Biomimicry Business Case Study: Sharklet Technologies, Inc.* Biomimicry Advisory Services, 2015.

THE BLACKOUT AND THE BEE – ENCYCLE

Our greatest weakness lies in giving up.
The most certain way to succeed is always to try just one more time.

– Thomas Edison

If there is one question common to all businessmen and women, it is probably, "What will make my business successful?" Of course, the answer is: it depends.

Mark Kerbel and Roman Kulyk were a couple of wickedly astute guys with backgrounds in computer science and computer engineering along with an ample dose of energy knowledge stirred into their technological know-how. When they began working together, they didn't know much biology, much less anything about the tool of biomimicry. They did know a fair bit about ant and bee societies because they had read Steven Johnson's book *Emergence*,[1] which details the sources, history of and uses for emergent system principles. These principles, loosely explained, are the processes and resulting outcomes of individuals or individual units completing simple directives which, in combination, form larger more complex results. The result itself could be resources gathered, as with bees gathering nectar and pollen; a completed structure like an ant hill; a process of moving from one place to another, as with a flock of birds; or all of these.

They found these premises both engaging and interesting relative to business possibilities they were considering. Even so, the principles related to emergent systems hadn't applied to the first company they had started, a software company, even after working late nights and weekends to see how they could fit. So they parked the idea. The two men were looking for real-world problems to solve – particularly challenges presented in the use and management of energy – and effective tools to make any resulting business they might create successful.

Then came the blackout of 2003 in the Northeastern U.S. and Ontario, Canada. Over the next two days, 50 million people around parts of eight U.S. states and Southeastern Canada came to be able to imagine life before the assault of machines when, even in the Northeast, skies were starry by night and crystalline by day. But the blackout in our modern era, when machines have replaced tasks once done by hand, meant everything in the entire region ground to a halt. Lights remained dark. Drinking water slowed to a standstill in its pipes. Cash registers ceased their blue-lit ciphering. As Mark considered the jarring change that August night, he suddenly felt a kind of buzz – their course was clear. They needed to improve resilience in cities by improving the energy grid or at least energy efficiency. The stars seemed to shine down in accord.

But both men were adamant that resilience and sustainability shouldn't and, in fact, couldn't be the driver of what the ultimate product or service was. Although Mark was personally attracted to the concepts of sustainability, neither of them felt they should espouse those principles to their customer base. Sustainability must stand on its own. What they did want to do was to make sustainability financially beneficial to clients by managing energy usage – a kind of détente among the head, heart, and gut. They and their customers would do well by doing good.

The two began examining various energy challenges facing companies around the globe. As each new idea popped up, they would research it and ultimately discard it or find themselves moving into a space where they found the challenge connected to something else needing additional research. After a short while, they realized they could spend their lives researching with not much to show for it. Shaking their heads, they printed up what they had and threw the five main ideas which had materialized onto the table to mull and hopefully birth their next venture.

As they studied those five ideas, they realized the elements of real-world energy problems were all related to energy usage, energy savings, and energy generation or cost. It was as if a lightbulb of evidence kept illuminating the three concepts. Further focus was needed to break down an energy problem into the smaller pieces of energy control, or at least energy management – the latter of which seemed to be an ideal fit.

As Mark recounted, that's when they thought, "Wait a minute! If we go back to those emergent principles of bees and ants we read about a few years ago, could we use those behaviors to address these problems?"

Emergence and the swarm-based algorithms they observed in bees and ants might actually work as the vehicle for their business. They had unknowingly moved through the back of the wardrobe and into the realm of biomimicry. But, they thought, this was a crazy idea either someone had already disproved or surely someone was already doing it. After conducting further research into the matter, they realized no one had and no one was. Their company, REGEN, was born.

$$\approx$$

At this point in the story, it behooves us to gain a better understanding of how emergence works. Emergent behavior is rooted in nature and a look there can yield the most logical snapshot of how emergent systems actually function. Emergent behavior is a blend of order and anarchy which achieves a goal or set of goals through self-organized systems based on a feedback and pattern detection process. Social insects such as bees and ants are the most frequent species referred to in discussions about this practice. Organisms like these display emergent behaviors in an elegant, ever-evolving community building dance.

In bee or ant societies, a large number of individuals have a few, very simple commands programmed into their biological systems. Any particular bee or ant might be heeding a biochemical directive to "collect food." In the course of doing so, the individual also communicates something about the instruction through behavior or in a biochemically based fashion to other individuals upon randomly meeting them during the work day. As more individuals carrying the same directive meet and begin the same behavior, the signal is strengthened. (This is what you see when you notice a chorus line of ants promenading down your window ledge.)

All these signals are translatable to mathematics at their core. Bees, for example, are innately aware of the sun and its location, gravity, and, in the case of food gathering, distance to the source. Even elements like wind have an effect on their communication. The research Mark and Roman had read suggested upon finding food and returning to the hive that bees communicate by performing a dance – the direction, speed, and length of which can be translated into exact algorithmic maps for other bees to follow.

When food supplies reach an acceptable level, individuals recognize this and begin conveying a different message – that the larder is full – at which point each individual sets off to satisfy an equally simple set of directions to start afresh on a different task. As each does, its biochemical communication feedback loop transfers this new message to subsequent hive or hillmates it meets – resulting in a greater number of individuals addressing the work and the subsequent completion of this brand new task.

These commands don't come from a central ruling party like a queen. Internal biological programming blends with biochemical communication among random individuals and combines with the uncanny ability to form larger patterns. As these organisms progress, they experience and in fact depend on those random encounters with fellow hive or colony members which collectively begin to create such patterns. The greater the number of individuals performing a task, the stronger the pattern becomes, until it reaches the desired levels for project completion. These processes result in filled food banks, waste carried elsewhere, and living quarters constructed all in the most optimized forms and patterns.

Simple instructions plus random meetings with feedback loops, create evolving connected patterns also recognized and managed in a kind of self-organizing system. This results in a nearly perfect communication–action blend of many creatures acting in concert. Such are the governances of many social insects as well as schooling fish and even slime molds. The relatively simple interactions among these organisms create larger and more complex operating systems which support the entire species. Mark and Roman recognized nature's algorithms for these behaviors can be mimicked and adapted by humans by transforming them into mathematical formulas for purposes such as managing energy.

$$\approx$$

78 THE BLACKOUT AND THE BEE – ENCYCLE

Commercial electrical customers with larger buildings are generally charged for not only what they consume but also their peak demand. This means that often the highest 15-minute burst of usage the meter displays in a month, or variations on that theme, drives the cost of electric bills. Knowing large buildings require multiple heating and cooling units, Mark and Roman asked themselves, "Could we use an emergent, swarm-based algorithm here?"

As they worked, the concept evolved. Though the pair had little biological background, they both had a great general scientific curiosity and lest we forget, their knowledge of emergence. Originally, they looked at using the algorithm for pumps and motors; heating, ventilation, and air conditioning (HVAC) systems; and other types of energy loads, but the more they kept narrowing it down, the more logical individual HVAC sensors became as an innovation target.

Each ant or bee is "aware" of its job at any given moment. Over time their entire system modulates to accommodate what the entire population experiences. Of course, there were still a number of questions, but Mark and Roman began designing and building a small electronic apparatus with a wireless transmitter. With one of these on each HVAC unit, the combined "swarm" could electronically spread out the equivalent of a bee's chemical pheromone trail to the rest of the colony. If each transmitter could "hear" other's "trails," then by modifying a swarming algorithm individual nodes could create a grand electrical scheme by communicating electronically with their neighbors, thereby controlling energy at any point in time in relation to all the other building's units. Just like ants and bees, each REGEN electrical transmitter modulated its behavior a little bit here and a little bit there – depending on what the other transmitters around the building communicated – to achieve the goal of coordinating to save energy.

There were, they knew, thousands and thousands of HVAC systems in every city ready, in their minds, to communicate and reduce energy loads. They now had a problem and a potential solution that seemed like it could work, but they were in for a shock as they sought support for their new way of problem-solving.

Mark approached researchers who were well versed in academia and often quoted in the realm of emergent behavior for a little reassurance, possible subsidiary thoughts on commercial applications for comparison, or even a little inspiration. When he contacted the first academic, he was told he didn't understand; this concept just wasn't ready for commercial or industrial use yet. More study was needed.

He was taken aback, but he and Roman had tested the algorithm on sample cases at the white-boarded proving ground in their offices. It was true they had run through a number of iterations and stumbled. But each time they did, they dissected their work and found a miscalculation was their foil – not a fault in the algorithm. Each time it looked like the algorithm wasn't going to work; they found it was their "stupid human tricks," as they took to calling them, taking them south. The algorithm worked.

When Mark went to a second scholar and encountered the same thing, he and Roman were somewhat amused thinking, "What? What do you mean?" They couldn't imagine why the scholars weren't more interested in their breakthrough.

With the third academic voicing a similar objection, Mark thought, "You know, OK, thank you for your comments and I appreciate your thoughts."

But he and his partner knew it had to be doable. It was just a matter of understanding the application. Although they didn't know it at the time, this was where they took another step in a typical biomimetic process. They began to examine the context and parameters needed for their industrial "organism" to survive. Did heat matter? Did cold matter? How could they protect the unit from rain and snow? "Let's just prove them wrong. Go ahead, you guys study it and we'll do it. And we'll tell you when we're done."

It wound up being an intellectual challenge as much as anything else, to prove to the supposed experts that – at least with what they knew so far – you didn't have to just keep studying it. There was enough information already available for REGEN to make something useful.

However, there was another challenge they had to surmount. When considering biomimicry and how nature works, it's a matter of doing what's needed with the least amount of materials and energy possible. This is often at odds with how a pre-biomimetic business world worked. To reap competitive advantage, designers and engineers had to and in many places still are required to keep adding features to products with little regard for the long-term benefits or costs of those additions promoting these features as "upgrades" and "new models." Mark and Roman were innovating counter to that pattern, with REGEN HVAC compact sensors having a very specific utility without a lot of add-ons.

Also, even if their product was materially and energy efficient, they also had to make their device fit easily into the existing HVAC work environment. They couldn't approach manufacturers and ask them to change *their* underlying engineering of a system even if manufacturers could then attach a sexy "new model" label to their product. That cost of time and money from outside vendors just wouldn't sell. If there was something they could drop into the system to have a specific positive effect on energy use and a financial return, then they'd have a chance.

The next group of naysayers was the bevy of technical, practical application energy experts who said, "No, it can't be done. That's not the way you manage energy loads." Sound familiar?

To be fair to them, maybe this wasn't the typical way humans have evolved to solve problems, but we are a young species with much to learn from other species around us having leagues more experience than we do. Nature knows a better way; and now the guys were fervently following the paths of emergent, swarming behaviors of bees and ants to move buildings toward energy efficiency. It took a lot of explanations, but ultimately, it all came down to results. That's the only way people would believe it.

So, they began to hone the application for what was becoming a small wireless device with the ability to communicate among fellow sensors to shave peak energy loads. They found the original device they designed wouldn't necessarily work for tall, thin buildings or small individual or individually connected buildings like strip malls. They would solve these problems with later iterations of the device. The original device *did* work well for low, wide buildings with multiple air conditioners sitting on rooftops. Theaters, big box retail, and other types of office or warehouse spaces with good-sized footprints to heat or cool and fairly big zones for each to cover would work well with their "swarming" assistance. The heating and cooling in these buildings was a larger chunk of overall costs, and the REGEN devices could yield a mighty bang for the buck.

The two kept heads bent toward managing energy consumption and perfected sensors that would talk to each other first to coordinate and shave loads – and later go further, automatically turning off devices not needed at specific times of day or under certain conditions.

Among their first customers was a family-owned theater chain in New Mexico. With the Southwest's challenge of managing extraordinary energy loads, especially in summer months, the company first elected to try the sensors at three facilities.

The sensors were easily installed and turned on while with Mark and Roman quietly monitored the theater's energy use behind the scenes to understand the base load. After a couple of weeks of learning the heating and cooling rhythms of the buildings, the two flipped the switches and began a savings course which ended up yielding $35,361 in energy savings for the first year. At the writing of this book, the owners of the company have since almost tripled their number of buildings with sensors guiding their energy use.

Next, they applied the technology to Sage Hill School, a high school with a wish to save energy while teaching students about energy management and an attendant dividend of investing funds saved into their environmental stewardship programs. The school shaved 28% off their consumption and reinvested that erstwhile expense into those student programs.

This success was followed by a contract with CCI, a pioneering valve production company known for its transformational technologies across 16 countries on five continents and counting. After applying REGEN's swarm-based units for demand, they amassed $25,000 in savings over just six months.

As time moved on, the pair moved forward gaining hundreds of companies as customers. Household names like Pier 1, Petco, and BMW became believers. Michaels, Sports Authority, and Sears joined in as the company sold thousands of units. Roman later moved on to other business pursuits while remaining friendly with Mark, who most recently served as Chief Technical Officer for REGEN, newly branded as Encycle.

As for biomimicry, a core group of people at the company keep it always in their minds as a design base. The business and sales people at Encycle are also well versed in the core principles which carried the company to where it is today. They know the swarm algorithm and know how to articulate how this is different from those used on conventional buildings. They continue to grow the company globally in places like Japan, for instance, where a food and beverage production and distribution company noted early demand energy savings of between 20% and 30%. Mark noted the additional value of biomimicry to his customers' corporate sustainability reports and added, "The whole biomimetic angle is what makes us uniquely successful."

When asked about the future, Mark kicked back and looked up at the sky – cloudy that day.

> I try to convince people more and more they should look at this (biomimicry) as part of a standard approach – part of their everyday toolkit. Actually, it bothers me that it's not part of the standard control system course in engineering. It should be.

It's good for Earth which is good for people and in the end makes good dollars and sense and ultimately yields success. It's a good way to make a living.

ENCYCLE LESSONS LEARNED

Understanding systems and context is critical to any solution-building landscape. Where does your company's energy originate? Where does it enter your facilities and how many buildings, vehicles, etc., do you have? How much do you use on average? When do your peak highs and lows take place and why? How are circumstances the same and different in locations and settings where you currently work and where you might expand?

The challenge for Mark and Roman became how to optimize energy systems with questions such as these very much in the foreground. In nature, efficiency with energy can mean not just the difference in saving resources or being comfortable but the difference between living and dying. Emergent behaviors in nature optimize energy intake and output throughout life while accomplishing all the day-to-day tasks required to eat, drink, seek or construct and maintain shelter, mate, and rear young. Instead of operating from a centralized command and control modality, organisms using emergent behaviors are decentralized in their operations. Here is some wisdom the pair learned from these organisms and the biomimetic business path they traveled.

Learning about various aspects of a business in partnership with others or discovering what you share in common relative to sustainability goals may help you find the "spark" that illuminates a business opportunity. Mark and Roman found it through a blackout, a book, and the theory/algorithms around emergence. Humans famously underscore competition as a major driver of society and, in fact, underscore it in nature as well. We intone thoughts of "survival of the fittest" while more often nature thrives on cooperation whether between or among animals, plants, fungi, and other organisms or some productive combination of these. *Collaboration with people and/or other natural partners having complementary backgrounds and common points of interest or challenges can yield your next successful business.* Addressing a challenge like what they had with energy generation, use and savings led the two to mimic the emergent tactics bees and ants use to solve their challenges. Discreet tasks, communication among units, and cyclic feedback patterns made it all work for creatures like ants and, as it turns out, businesses like Encycle.

Prototyping continued from the concept phase into the development phase in order to fine-tune and optimize saleable products. Third-party verification was achieved through a process created as part of a grant. *This underutilized financing method allowed crucial testing to take place in a finite time period under their control and for reasonable costs rather than relying on the changing and sometimes expensive landscapes often found with some commercial third-party verifiers.* Although they utilized government grants, the duo started with their own personal savings and, like Sharklet, angel investment. *Understanding the roles and possibilities for each of these income sources is key to attaining and coordinating them.*

Within the time period of testing and establishing credibility, receiving the input and backing of researchers and academics can provide a boost to businesses and, in some cases, is vital. Having stated that, inventions and/or business practices can be tested on their own, and subsequent business action plans can be (and have been) successful without such input. Many, like Encycle, can launch based on the success of internal testing and a few stalwart early adopters. Businesses can still benefit greatly from the support and input from academia and other experts. However, few product fields are completely dependent on them. *Results are the best proof.*

With all of that important preparation and testing in mind, it's crucial to remember sometimes in business it's time to simmer.

Sometimes it time to seize. *Be aware of the whispers in your mind that tell you, "There's something here," and pursue it.*

As we then move forward, whether it's during a business or product development path or simply working to create greater efficiencies in our work, *we need to understand the role sustainability and/or biomimicry and its cousins play in our work.* Mark and Roman wanted to accommodate their customers' needs and work to incorporate biomimicry and sustainability – not preach to their customers, hoping they would change. Here again, along with identifying the functions to be solved for, pinpointing context relative to potential clients is key to fitting a solution into their specific enterprises. *Whether incorporating a sustainable product or design into a setting, fitting it into the client's needs and processes is a central tenet to success.* Biomimicry can successfully be used as the base for design processes and later married with engineering practices. It can be applied to the communication, investing structures, or entirely different realms – but context is key.

Additionally, *when determining target markets think globally and act… at whatever scale works.* Although the pair began with direct sales, market analysis and testing revealed they would soon be able to move to account-level operations on an international scale. They also saw growth potential in retaining their position as an original equipment manufacturer.

Like nature, businesses evolve based on opportunistic and/or necessary adaptations. While Encycle started out with a primary aim to lower peak demand, they also came to recognize they could thrive in the arena of demand response management. They found their niche in buildings with at least four to six HVAC units. Because of this and their degree of effectiveness, the company deployed over 6,000 units in their first 11 years.[2]

Biomimicry can stand on its own as a business practice. As reflected in the real dollars saved by the companies who have deployed it, biomimicry is not just another pretty public relations (P.R.) face. However, as with any "green," "sustainable," or "regenerative" practice, the professional's intent must be authentic. The context should be examined and paired with appropriate partner expertise (whether human or not). And the financing and business plan should pair synergistically with all these elements.

ACKNOWLEDGMENTS

I want to express thanks to Mark Kerbel for his time and the extensive amount of information offered through interviews and e-mails beginning in March of 2015 without which this story would have never come to life. Mark was a man of enormous vision and action. He will be missed. −MF

REFERENCES

1 Johnson, Steven. *Emergence – The Connected Lives of Ants, Brains, Cities and Software*. New York, NY: Scribner, 2001.

2 Chirazi, J. *Biomimicry Business Intelligence – Financial & Market Research; Biomimicry Business Case Study: Encycle*. Biomimicry Advisory Services, 2015.

8

SO WHAT?

If a values-driven approach to business can begin to redirect this vast power toward more constructive ends than the simple accumulation of wealth, the human race and Planet Earth will have a fighting chance.

– Ben Cohen, cofounder Ben & Jerry's

Biomimicry and its cousins can be viewed and used the way the companies described here have done – as a tool for sustainability, human benefits, and enhanced business outcomes. Some of the companies intended to live more generously with all the other organisms on Earth as one immediate outcome. Their leaders recognized the reciprocity they were and are aiming for ultimately helps all living things be more resilient and flourish together. Business, people, and organisms from the wild do not exist in isolation after all. As Ray Anderson knew, we are braided together. At first blush it would seem this line of thought flies in the face of long-time survival of the fittest beliefs and treatises. However, as we are coming to learn, the world is more strongly guided by mutualism – the understanding that many organisms rely on interactions with other organisms in a mutually supporting manner to operate in a healthy manner or, indeed, exist at all. Ants provide protection to acacia trees from disease-causing agents and some nibbling plant eaters. In return, they receive food in the form of nectar from the tree and lodge within their thorns in return. We now know certain fungi around tree roots provide a means of enhanced water and nutrition supplies while receiving carbohydrates from the trees necessary for their survival. And human beings would be unable to digest our food were it not for the living bacteria in our gut, who in turn rely on our bodies for food and shelter. These types of mutually supporting partnerships aren't just nice. They're necessary.

Of course, the innovators in these pages were also looking for enhanced business outcomes. The bottom line, after all, has to be at least a substantial portion of the *bottom line* in order to stay in business. A company cannot build reciprocity with nature if a company doesn't exist. But in these pages we have seen immediate benefits to that bottom line through partnerships with nature. Interface immediately decreased waste costs when they ventured into using biomimicry as a tool. Encycle profited from lowering energy bills (and attendant resource use) for their customers. The ability of PAX lily impellers to circulate water on a massive scale with minute energy inputs, and Nike to improve air quality for employees with green rubber, helped bring these companies profit, reduce energy consumption, protect worker health, and enhance public images as well. With Sharklet's patterns yielding Foley catheters, central venous catheters, and endotracheal tubes, biomimicry has even started working to save lives by lowering infection rates while reducing the need for antibiotics. The effectiveness of these products has supported sales and increased profits in every case.

But what is the definition of profitability? Are we operating on the consumer-driven model or the broader global citizen-driven paradigm that takes quality of life into account on the front end? Can we go beyond just saving energy, waste, and material costs? Certainly air quality and reduced hospital acquired infections are an argument that, yes, we can and should!

Healthy profit and people along with environmental sustainability drive business. Profit is obvious, but environmental sustainability and social benefits are advancing quickly to the fore. The ancients, in this case the Greeks beginning with Aristotle, discussed economics as a continuum. Chrematistics lays at one end with its focus solely on the accumulation and management of money and an eye only toward short-term gain in dollars – in other words, the consumer-driven model. At the other end lays oikonomia, which deals not simply with money and its gain or loss but with stewardship and the responsibility we have to the entities around us.

88 SO WHAT?

This beneficial long view with both people and natural resources in mind is the global citizen-driven framework which provides stewardship for our larger, more inclusive community. We have skated away from and around that larger, essential community for too long. Many will glide for a bit and will continue to do more harm to people and the environment. Some will do less bad to both, but very few will move into the realm of reciprocity. Yet it is there – the beginnings of reciprocity. And when we front-load this notion of stewardship, many times it can magnify its benefits to the triple bottom line.

Humanity exists on a continuum from base depravity to enlightened and visionary actions. Wherever a person or company exists on that continuum, they can always evolve. Some may never be leaders – in ingenuity or anything else. Still, they likely contribute in some ways to the community in which they reside – perhaps through volunteering or donating to a good cause. Other business leaders will be aspirational, advancing their business, their field of endeavor, and the whole of their community – human and nonhuman – in a variety of ways and measures. In business, as with any other continuum, the grand majority maintain residence somewhere in the middle. If we were assigning a grade, many would take home a B, C, or D. Although for many people C's and D's are untenable, we should remember they indicate "Average" and "Below Average" – not "Failing".

However, some companies are failing. Some ignore the triple bottom line and/or reciprocity completely. They do earn a failing grade. Some use the triple bottom line as subterfuge for good public relations. As shocking as this may be, we should be aware of this practice of greenwashing. It exists. Most of us know it and all should steer clear. Honesty is the obvious reason for that. If that is not a value within a company, leaders should also understand what happens to a brand if the public discovers their ploy.

Some company leaders allow themselves to be guided by profit above all else either for their own coffers or to satisfy their investors and boards. Even though some of them contribute to good causes or embrace some type(s) of positive environmental or social action, their continued negative actions in either or both realms so far outweigh the positives that we rightly tag them with this greenwashing label – or decry, boycott, and/or protest against them for not caring at all. Often it is difficult to determine which is worse. Greenwashing, like poorly applied bleach, discolors the entire wash load. But not caring at all plummets us down the stewardship mountain like a luge with no breaks. Companies, however, can choose evolution along the continuum toward a triple bottom-line success and reciprocity. Most simply haven't chosen to do so at this point. Fortunately, more companies are beginning that evolution, and more consumer and industry groups are devising indices to let buyers know what "grades" companies are earning. Hopefully, customers will refer to these guides in ever-increasing numbers and do their own research to drive their purchases and practices – applying pressure in at least some sectors.

Many companies step onto the continuum toward reciprocity with all human and nonhuman organisms but tiptoe lightly as they go. I once had the pleasure to work with a multinational corporation with a factory in a drought-stricken water catchment doubly impacted by sprawl. They were paying tens of thousands of dollars to convey water, after treating it twice, to the city for final treatment where it was then discharged only to run immediately out of that catchment area. Since the only element left in the water was non-toxic and inert as it left the factory, the company wanted assistance with getting the proper permits to transfer the water to a neighboring golf course pond. The company would definitely save money, but the golf course also gained a steady stream of water as did the catchment area. Mutualism! I was thrilled to help, but when I asked if I could laud them in public, they immediately declined. Why?

"Environmentalists will pat us on the back for this but then look for everything we're doing wrong. We don't need that."

Every company, if graded fairly, will not earn an A or at least will not do so consistently. It is critical we recognize and applaud positive steps (if they are genuine and do not appear as a single effort) just as we continue to discourage and change the negative. The labeling of companies merely as good or bad or falsely accusing them of greenwashing is both irresponsible and counterproductive. Thankfully, unless we have been abused or are infirm in some way, all of us have a level of ambition to almost always strive to be better. According to Abraham Maslow's hierarchical ladder,[1] "better" can have an array of meanings but in essence falls between a base of attaining physiological comfort and safety on up to higher levels where we gain security, love, acceptance, and self-actualization. Self-actualization includes not just benefits to self but benefits beyond self. Are you seeing a pattern emerge? As business leaders, we need to profit in order to gain those lower levels of safety and comfort found through our companies' continued existence. Some would argue profit even drives a number of the higher levels like self-esteem. But self-actualization, the highest rung on the ladder, only occurs after the full complement of lower rungs is attained. This is where long-term thinking about the company as part of a community-building reciprocity exists among our own and other organisms. It requires a base of monetary profit, but as the ancients reflected through oikonomia, it also requires stewardship and works in mutualistic partnership with the world outside its doors as well. This is not just to supply the business with a means to an end but to take action on behalf of people and the natural world for their own sake.

We can enter this space of stewardship and reciprocity out of guilt or greed or fear. We can also move to it through benevolence and aspiration. With regard to the former, a number of books have been written about proverbial environmental canaries in coal mines. Climate change and its negative effects on business as well as human populations and a wide array of other plants, animals, and organisms are real. We are also beginning to recognize that, because of natural resource overuse, we are additionally looking at serious scarcity threats to specific chemical elements like zinc, helium, and silver *within the next hundred years.*[2] These data are the result of research and information from entities like the National Aeronautics and Space Administration, the National Oceanic and Atmospheric Administration, the Chemistry Innovation Knowledge Transfer Network, and the American Chemical Society. Negative effects from changing climate and future element scarcity are only two examples of environmental indicators, among many. According to the World Economic Forum's Global Risks Report 2020, a full array of business risks will begin to materialize in areas such as construction, energy, fashion, and textiles, which are among the sectors especially vulnerable to ecological destruction.[3] In addition to billions of dollars' worth of disturbance to particular industries, increased flooding from the loss of protection attributed to coral reefs and mangroves will cost businesses in flooding and increased insurance costs. These realities are likely already affecting your business in some ways, either obliquely or directly, and they definitely will in the coming years.

So much for fear! The other way we can move forward is to take the self-actualizing long view, which can result in increased profits, but also long-term stewardship and sustainability. This requires us to have those as intentional goals and embrace a readiness to evolve in actions as well as ideas. With this in mind, we can examine our base of operations – Earth. Earth is a closed-loop system. We prosper best if we recognize that and strive to operate in accordance with it. Within our closed-loop system, we exist as part of a construct we refer to as nature. It is critical to accept the difference of existing as *a part of* and not *apart from* nature. Once we do this, directional choices at work can crystallize, and a myriad of opportunities open up to us including the world of biomimicry and its cousins.

Why do companies use biomimicry or its relatives? Some do it simply to accomplish a task or fill out another line on their corporate sustainability report if one exists. But once they have used the methods, most companies use it as a form of adaptation because it has worked and/or their leadership respects the natural resources required to do business or values the nature of nature itself. Organisms and the systems which they comprise (yes, including humans) are by far and away the most capable designers and engineers on the planet. If we can design as they design, within the physical, biological, and chemical boundaries that govern the planet, we can prosper as these companies are. If we design in opposition to them, or more generally Earth's systems, we will ultimately fail. Witness the ephemeral properties of any industry over the course of human existence on Earth. Compare it to the resilience of mosses or alligators. Whose strategies have caused less harm and allowed for flourishing populations over millennia?

We regularly examine and are familiar with our own company challenges and procedures for addressing them. If we examine the approaches companies in this book and their biom★ colleagues have taken to imitate nature, we note we too can choose a similar path. By identifying the functional challenges we face, then observing the ways nature solves for the same function, and emulating that, we can achieve greater energy and material efficiency with less toxicity to nature, including ourselves and everyone around us. If we find ourselves responding and adapting to the various physical, chemical, and biological boundaries of the world, we can land in a place called "balance" that ever-undulating realm with nevertheless distinct boundaries. How do we know when we've passed boundaries? Away from the office we know we've passed some boundaries when we venture too close to a volcano or climb mountains beyond our capacity to breathe effectively. Recognizing our relationship with heat or oxygen in these cases is very clear. However, when we're not standing in front of a volcano, running our business far away from immediate harm, we often exceed these bounds of balance since lava isn't in the process of burning our feet. Because of this lack of immediate damage and, as important, because we are still fairly unfamiliar with ways of measuring harmful or wasteful outcomes from our work, we many times stubbornly reason our way into "solutions" that ignore the larger canvas of balance with and economies of nature. As a result, businesses can and often do use additional energy, materials, harmful processes, etc., to achieve business survivorship in our man-made extended boundaries. Sometimes this survivorship temporarily bolsters esteem or profit, but if we venture into this space for too long, it will eventually divert us into decline.

In companies using biomimicry, bio-inspiration, or some of the other cousins effectively, we see certain attitudes and practices that have led them toward reciprocity and financial success. An enlightened leader doggedly pursued a restorative relationship with nature along with staff and leadership who embraced that same kinship. That persistence and continued evolution have been key at Interface. PAX has leaders who understand and *want to understand* the natural world and further strive to optimize work within Earth's operational rules and geometries. Nike has integrated biom* as one of a suite of sustainability tools and has identified staff with biological backgrounds to work with design staff to overcome prickly problems. Sharklet discovered using force is not always the answer. They prospered not from killing problematic bacteria but by recognizing what organisms need for survival and simply depriving them of it. They embraced a radically new way of problem-solving and adopted nature's elegant solutions which work better than elevating heat, escalating pressure, or adding more chemicals to resolve a challenge. Leadership at Encycle refused to be deterred or derailed by negativity or disbelief. Like others here, they encountered those who said, "It won't work." "That's not how you do it." "It's not ready." They knew results are the best proof.

Have they achieved reciprocity or a restorative end game? Not yet. Materials science has not evolved enough at this point to allow for much product generation with completely benign components and distribution practices that are mutualistic. What's more, few have adopted habitat protection practices to offset outputs or outcomes from said operational practices. Have they decided their businesses should stop growing at some point to benefit the natural world? One would be hard pressed to answer that in the affirmative. They have, however, taken one critical step. They have each stepped onto a continuum of care where they are decidedly striving to be better each day – not just for profit – but for planet and people as well. Are biomimicry and its cousins leading us toward reciprocity? In these companies and others where the intent is combined with nature's strategies, design integration and engineering expertise they are on the road.

Here, after reading these stories, we can also answer our initial questions regarding business.

- Are they experiencing success with biom★ and has it been measured? Yes, they are measurably reducing waste and energy use which is saving money. They are creating entire businesses based on helping people avoid infection and/or positively impacting health and therefore the bottom line in hospitals, factories, and communities. And as a side benefit, as with PAX, they are solving additional problems toward which they were not even originally aiming.
- How was biom★ introduced to the company? Janine Benyus and Dayna Baumeister illuminated or underscored the practice of biomimicry for leaders of Interface and Nike. Designers at Nike also headed the early charge at that company. In the case of PAX, Jay's love for and study of nature from a young age planted the seed. At Sharklet and Encycle, a lightbulb moment and both scientists' and entrepreneurs' persistence gave rise to products.
- Was it scaled up and is there likelihood of scaling up in other companies? Yes and yes. In fact, we have already seen biom★ embraced in an ever larger number of companies and in laboratories where it has led to new practices and products as well as entirely new businesses. Blue Planet emulates coral's use of CO_2

to create cement capable of sequestering carbon. Ornilux mimics the ultraviolet reflective qualities of some spiders' webs to reduce bird strikes against windows by over 70%. Evologics looked to dolphin communication methods with frequency emissions able to identify underwater earthquakes. Dozens of other examples exist in the realms of packaging, propulsion, energy generation, and building design, among many others.

- Where are the speed bumps? You've read about speed bumps that have been overcome – naysayers, requirements for testing, and marrying these technologies into existing design or engineering frameworks. However, as you have seen, the impediments for these companies were eventually all surmounted.

Many companies of every ilk fail each year – many with radical new ideas and a plethora just doing the same old thing with a different name. Whether they deploy biomimicry specifically or biom* in their business or not, businessmen and women must still comply with solid, informed business practices. As we look at businesses where biomimicry hasn't "stuck," it rarely has been because biomimicry didn't work. Instead, it has been for the usual reasons innovations fail to lodge in a company's organizational DNA or standard operating procedures; namely, things like:

- Lack of knowledge about the details required of and for a specific innovation (which is often linked to not fully understanding the problem itself at a functional level)
- Lack of knowledge, skills, or capital required to integrate the innovation into the company or marketplace
- Lack of a champion inside the company
- Failure to measure the innovation's effects appropriately (or at all)
- Failure to capitalize effectively or to a scalable level

Of course, there is also the chance a specific biomimetic solution is simply unattainable at the time of application for functional, physical, or chemical design and engineering reasons. Even biologists working with a business team might not always fully understand the biological strategies of organisms being studied because humans haven't yet unlocked the secrets of that particular organism or its system. This is one of the reasons habitat protection is so vital. Even if we don't protect our oceans, prairies, and forests for reciprocity, we can learn little from organisms who no longer exist.

The success of biomimicry and biom★ innovation and adoption depends on learning and applying biom★ methods, but also requires the elements of proper integration into existing business systems, measurement of subsequent successes or failures along with a lack of negative outcomes just like any business tool. Applying a new practice can cause anxiety at first to be sure. But ultimately companies can achieve increased profits through decreased waste, material and energy use, and/or reduced or eliminated use of toxic chemicals, while they increase profits if they choose to enter into some form of biom★. And they can move further toward oikonomia if they engage in some type of reciprocity with nature. Many companies using biom★ also discover those positive ripple effects solving additional problems. PAX's lily impeller wasn't originally designed for the purpose of deterring freezing in water storage tanks, but that's what happens. Sharklet is expanding use of its texture into new solution areas such as reducing secondary infections in cataract repair with new intraocular lenses. Interface is now looking at their entire campuses in an effort to make factories operate like forests. But it can all start with something as simple as identifying a function needing to be solved for, walking outside, and asking, "How would nature…?"

Biomimicry and biom★ in general can serve business by making and saving money, enhancing environmental sustainability in the world around us, and helping increase our resilience to an array of business, environmental, and social challenges. Toxicity from formaldehyde motivated Columbia Wood Products to create wood glue without formaldehyde by mimicking underwater adhesion properties of mussels to build better plywood. Energy needs drove BPS bioWAVE to transform wave energy into electricity through a pumping system built to sway back and forth in imitation of bull kelp. These solutions and more have depended on a partner from nature. Thankfully for Sharklet, sharks still exist although over six dozen species are threatened or endangered.[4] Mountain goats require specific isolated habitats for their survival. Bees and other pollinators' numbers have suffered terribly from an array of ills — both natural and man-made; and many populations have experienced precipitous declines. Plants, fungi, and an assortment of other organisms have

96 SO WHAT?

been extirpated as humans have destroyed or denigrated habitats in which they live. If this was a book on morality, we could insert several chapters on these topics alone. After all, don't these organisms have an inalienable right to live? But this is a book on business, so while you personally may consider these questions in moral terms, all businessmen and women should consider them from the viewpoint of partnership. We can't partner with them if they don't exist.

So, what? Well, now you have the knowledge you can choose to go ahead. Go to work. Make a living. Learn from physical, chemical, and operational boundaries surrounding us and the living organisms, our fellow planetary citizens, with whom we share this place. Engage them in partnerships. Whether those relationships are biophilic or bioinspired alone or are fully biomimetic, you can operate with a longer view toward all our offspring's' futures. Reading this book may have been your first step, but as you read on, you will discover a host of additional steps you and your company can take on your own journey across the continuum of care.

REFERENCES

1 Maslow, A. H. "A Theory of Human Motivation". *Psychological Review*, 50, No. 4 (1943), 370–396.

2 Royal Society of Chemistry. "A Sustainable Global Society". Chemical Sciences and Society Summit White Paper. Cambridge, UK: RSC, 2011.

3 The World Economic Forum. *The Global Risks Report 2020*. January 15, 2020.

4 International Union of Concerned Scientists. "A Quarter of Sharks and Rays Threatened with Extinction". https://www.iucn.org/content/a-quarter-sharks-and-rays-threatened-extinction. January 2014. Accessed 20 November, 2019.

NOW WHAT?

All successful networking is dependent on two key things: reciprocity and curiosity.[1]

– Phyllis Weiss Haserot, Author, *You Can't Google It!*

The "now what" depends on you. What are your intentions and what are your needs? How do you define "making a living"?

So much of what we face in the world today is distressing at best. Inequities based on income, race, and culture plague us. We are alarmed by the loss of wildlife species at levels many times higher than our natural extinction curves. And climate change with all its attendant ills of sea-level rise, increased drought, storm intensities, and a changing biosphere reveals itself to increasing numbers of people in ways ever more difficult to ignore. These things, considered separately or especially as a whole, can sometimes freeze our ability to work proactively or at least create a seemingly unassailable fog of malaise. Indeed, many of us admit to being at a complete loss throwing our hands up in despair crying out, "What can I do? I'm only one person!"

Author Barry Lopez answered the question from his perspective as he spoke with fellow writer, Robert Macfarlane,[2] about how people in the future will consider our actions affecting the earthly and atmospheric challenges we face today and what he feels we now must do,

The opportunity is to face up to it... The question is what are we going to do now and the answer is learn a language so we can learn how to speak to each other so that we don't leave each other in profound, existential loneliness because we are unable to say what we can't bear. We need a language that will allow us to discuss the next generation and the next. What are we going to leave them?

Biomimicry and its cousins are forms of such a language – a language of structures, processes, and systems formed across billions of years whose strategies are waiting for us to deploy in our offices, factories, and communities. Equally if not more importantly, these cousins make up a language of hope, inclusivity, and potential reciprocity. By observing and working to comprehend the strategies used by other species, then emulating them in the best ways we can while seeking to do better with each iteration, we have an opportunity to build better, to work better, and to live better in a space of collaboration with fellow species. Lopez continued,

> What we are facing now in the Anthropocene, is the responsibility to develop a language we've never spoken before, master it and use it to keep ourselves strong while we deal with all of these things like climate change.

CREATING A NEW LANGUAGE AND INTENTIONS

So, what are our intentions? Do we come of age, choose a job or profession solely to make money, and hopefully enjoy our job (or at least not despise it) along the way? We stand at the threshold of two schools of action. My father was a good man. As you read, he followed his parents' way of supporting his family and engaging with community. But we live in a new day with critical challenges not just to and for ourselves, our businesses, or our countries, but to the planet we and others all inhabit. When we are forming our intentions in business, we can try to continue planning and working in the older ways wrought in the thrall of the Industrial Revolutions. We also have the opportunity and actually the need to do as Mr. Lopez suggests with regard to our challenges and "face up to it."

Creating a new language can create new business pathways and opportunities. That new language begins with intention. Creating intention begins with asking ourselves a few honest questions. Instead of beginning, as we often have been taught, with,

"What are my goals in life?"
Let's begin instead with,
"What are my intentions in life?"

What's the difference? A goal is the direct announcement or planned effort – whether written, spoken, or thought – usually resulting in some sort of external manifestation. Intentions, on the other hand, are the determination to act in a certain way. Intentions activate our values. Without going into the zone of psychology (which is a different book), let's go right back to Mr. Lopez by asking ourselves,

> How do I want to behave in business? What are my intentions and do they conflict with those I have for my overall life? Do they conflict with the well-being of others?

At this point we can choose whether our values exist solely for the benefit to ourselves, our families, and our companies or extend beyond those to include our human and nonhuman neighbors whose communities are an inescapable part of our larger world. Let's say, since you've read this far, your intentions include creating profit while benefitting people and planet. You now have a foundation for your goals and can ask,

> What are going to be the goals I adopt to activate those intentions (values)?

Go ahead. Give it a go. Scribble some of your intentions and a few goals to activate them.

Notes:

Consider sticking to Earth's rules and finding new partners.

100 NOW WHAT?

Next, since we know our intentions and goals, we can ask ourselves,

How do I get there? What is my action plan?

Here is some room to brainstorm a little more.

> *Notes:*

Biomimicry and biom★ in general originate in the natural world, that is to say THE world. We have often failed to consider the totality of THE world in business, but as you now know, it is a place with finite boundaries. As we have learned, it has specific rules of operation and strategies to deal with all its challenges in a manner supporting individuals and entire systems cooperatively. It is this place in which we conduct our work. As the signs say, "There is no Planet B" at least for now. So when we consider how to activate our intentions and goals, we should intelligently consider the rules and principles that drive this planet. (See Chapter 3.) With these as a starting place, we can now ask,

To what degree will I act to sync up with these conditions?

Here is where you can brainstorm a little to match actions you've written with potential start-up zones. Conserving water? Energy? Reducing material use or waste? A combination of these? Which of these starting zones would work best for your firm?

> *Notes:*

The level of cooperation we have known in business and in the world thus far is, and I mean this both poetically and tangibly, nothing compared to what it might be if we grasp the partnerships offered to us by and through nature. If we include and treat those potential partnerships synergistically in our goals instead of slicing out parts or adding in odd portions later, these relationships can yield insights, opportunities, and results greater than we can achieve by simply adding in a sustainable practice here and there. These partnerships hold the power to move business from a destructive space to a position of doing less bad, becoming sustainable, and finally morphing into a place of restoration, regeneration, and reciprocity – if we embrace those into our intentions and work to make them a reality. It has begun working in a number of businesses already storied here.

We have walked out of caves and into lives of relative convenience and abundance in many places around the globe. It is therefore not unreasonable at all to think we can take a next step and extend that abundance to all our fellow humans and beyond – to the other organisms with which we share Earth. We do not have to do this out of nobility, although we have shown we sometimes have that in us. We can do it from a position of practicality. It is, in fact, practical to consult nature because, ultimately, it is necessary. We know it as we examine our dinner plates where one of every three bites of food arrives courtesy of pollinators. We know it from the results of microorganisms breaking down decaying matter to create the soil that grows our food. We know it from recognizing other organisms put food on our plates, clothes on our backs, and a roof over our heads. Nature, including all the organisms and the physical components comprising it, allows us to exist and carry on our lives. So as we determine how to activate our intentions and goals, how might we take responsibility to shore up the piers of our existence? We can ask,

> How do I consult and partner with nature to activate my intentions and accomplish my goals?

As you have read, leaders like Ray Anderson, Jay Harman, Dr. Anthony Brennan, and an increasing number of professionals are defining what problems they need to solve and breaking them down into functional language while considering their basic intentions.

> How do I cover a floor?
> How do I build a fan?
> How do I create a surface that foils organisms when they try to attach?
> Then they make a simple substitution by asking,
> How would nature do that?

In conjunction with those questions, each leader and their teams stepped out into nature – whether the woods, the bay, or the beach to observe for themselves how nature would tackle their challenges.

For each individual and each company, the path toward biomimicry, biom*, and the responsible problem-solving to which they contribute may be very different. Some entrepreneurs, designers, engineers, or those in business departments seeking a better, more responsible way to do business will start by defining a problem and asking that question of nature. Others, like the designer of the Shinkansen bullet train, observe nature regularly and eagerly to see what unique and useful things it can do which can be applied to their work.

OVERCOMING INERTIA AND OTHER HOBGOBLINS

As we move forward, we will also regularly need to tackle the inertia born out of business as usual. We may encounter it before this step or sometimes afterward, but rest assured overcoming inertia will require our energy at some point in the process. Many times this involves examining or reexamining our own intentions, goals, planned actions, and starting zones. When we feel secure in those, we might simply begin by collecting and studying biom* examples of success such as those in this book. Then we might look for opportunities to act similarly in our workplace. If we are not company leaders, we will need to examine the pathways to our leaders, which have yielded change in the past and consider if those might be plausible for our next steps.

Once you have selected one or more routes to take your ideas to your leaders, be prepared. As you begin the journey, there will probably be other hobgoblins you have to confront and smite. Whether in yourself, bosses, teammates, and/or employees, you may have to overcome the fear of being wrong. When dealing in innovation and invention, the act of being wrong is often an ingredient which must be added into a recipe to finally spawn success. In short, being wrong can aid you in being right. Try not to be afraid of it. Sometimes, as the leaders of these companies would tell you, one has to be wrong a number of times before success can finally be claimed. Still, knowing this is rarely enough to hold fear on the other side of the door. So, we must confront it again and again. That was one of the tools Ray Anderson brought to his team. He applied support and had faith in his team even when they made mistakes. They responded and then succeeded.

There is the hobgoblin of meeting people where they are. That usually begins with questions to find out where those people see challenges – whether they are clients, employees, teammates, or the boss. (That challenge space may be a completely different place for others than it is for us.) It also means we need to limit our own professional jargon. We will need to learn the languages of other professions or even other sectors of our own profession and hierarchical levels within our own companies in order to collaborate effectively with them. Communicating well can open doors of opportunity as successfully as the lack of it can shut them tight. As Jay Harman would remind us though, even when we communicate clearly, people might not respond with what we need. That doesn't mean we have to put our ideas and plans away. It simply means when we require the expertise of others in practices melding nature and

104 NOW WHAT?

knowledge of it to our problems, we should go out and get that expertise while communicating as clearly as we can. And we should attempt to take our partners' perspectives, languages, needs, and experiences into account.

Commonly we will seek the assistance of design, engineering, and business professionals, all of whom speak their own languages. In addition to those knowledgeable folks, we would be well served to also consult biologists. They are the authorities on organisms, how they operate, and, importantly, how their strategies operate. Ideally, you'll be communicating and learning the languages of a combination of all those groups to create a wellspring from which you can extract a solution which is both effective and regenerative.

You may also encounter the hobgoblin of greenwashing. This can mean confronting the intent or actual practice of greenwashing (whether in your own company or a partner's) or the fear of being accused of it. Certainly, it means recognizing the difficulties of overcoming wholesale traditional thinking and behaviors which can produce it. Remind yourself and others of what is at stake and what opportunities are present when we observe and mimic nature as accurately as possible. Putting lipstick on a pig does neither you nor the pig any good at all.

Finally, no matter what our background, expertise, and current roles are, we must cease digging into "right" and "wrong" as absolutes when we have a continuum of care onto which we can step. As an example, one might consider the companies in this book. Not all of them stepped right into the practice of biomimicry. In fact, most if not all of these companies began with bio-inspiration. Some of them are currently also engaged in bio-utilization, while other companies are using bionics, biophilia, and BioTRIZ, but they are all moving toward the regenerative end of the continuum at some level. They may not all move to the point of reciprocity – but they have begun the journey to do well by doing good.

That is one of the most critical aspects of working in the realm of biom*. As we have learned, the path is slightly (or greatly) different for each individual and/or each company. Even though teaching frameworks exist for biomimicry or BioTRIZ or any of the others, the practices may be mixed and matched. One company may emulate only the structures of nature, while other companies may move toward mimicking processes or entire systems. Some may achieve circularity where waste from one area is used to power another in a self-supporting cycle. Hopefully, many will form intentions to do business in a circular fashion, but some may not. The path you and your business take will be unique and reflect the challenges you have, the components of the practices you have chosen, the order in which you apply them, the level of transparency you embrace, your willingness to adapt and evolve, your personal capacity, and, foundationally, your intentions. Regardless of a company's particular combination of ingredients, you can move toward reciprocity on the continuum of care by applying biomimicry and biom★ in the way that best fits your company.

Defining a problem and asking the functional question(s) connecting it to and with nature can be a start if you have or are overcoming the inertia contained around business as usual. You've learned from the men and women in these pages and arrived at a starting point – only a start but a good one. These companies have embarked on their own continuums of care and so can you. In fact, if you've read the book to this point, you've already taken a positive first step. Forward motion from here can move in several directions.

Read another book. Sometimes, when we learn a new concept, it can be overwhelming enough (or intriguing enough) that we simply feel the need to learn more. If this is you, a number of options exist. You can read one or more of these fine books or a number of others:

Biomimicry: Innovation Inspired by Nature by Janine Benyus
iSites: Biomimetic Nature Journaling for Biomimicry by Erin Rovalo
The Shark's Paintbrush by Jay Harman
Biomimicry in Architecture by Michael Pawlyn
Teeming: How Superorganisms Work Together to Build Infinite Wealth on a Finite Planet (and Your Company Can Too) by Tamsin Woolley-Barker
The Nature of Business: Redesigning for Resilience by Giles Hutchins
The Nature of Investing: Resilient Investment Strategies through Biomimicry by Katherine Collins
Thinking in Systems: A Primer by Donella Meadows
Emergence: The Connected Lives of Ants, Brains, Cities and Software by Steven Johnson
Mid-Course Correction: Toward a Sustainable Business Model: The Interface Model by Ray Anderson

106 NOW WHAT?

The Ecology of Commerce by Paul Hawken

Ishmael by Daniel Quinn

The Nature Fix by Florence Williams

The Biophilia Hypothesis by Stephen Kellert

Birthright: People and Nature in the Modern World by Stephen Kellert

Biomimicry for Optimization, Control, and Automation by Kevin M. Passino

The Sustainability Champion's Guidebook – How to Transform Your Company by Bob Willard

Resilience: Why Things Bounce Back by Andrew Zolli and Ann Marie Healy

The Hidden Life of Trees by Peter Wohlleben

Fantastic Fungi: How Mushrooms Can Heal, Shift Consciousness, and Save the Planet edited by Paul Stamets

Bulletproof Feathers: How Science Uses Nature's Secrets to Design Cutting-Edge Technology by Robert Allen

Biologically Inspired Design: Computational Methods and Tools edited by Ashok Goel, Daniel A. McAdams and Robert B. Stone

Comparative Biomechanics: Life's Physical World – Second Edition by Steven Vogel

Life in Moving Fluids: The Physical Biology of Flow – Revised and Expanded Second Edition by Steven Vogel

Cats' Paws and Catapults: Mechanical Worlds of Nature and People by Steven Vogel

Biomechatronics by Marko B. Popovic

Fortunately, biomimicry and biom*, in general, have been around long enough that you can also go further by accessing a number of organizations and businesses with information to help you as you develop questions and the potential pathways you need for your next steps in one or more of these practices. Each person's route toward sustainability, regenerative practices, and/or reciprocity will be different. But whether you are an employee of a larger company, an entrepreneur, or a CEO, you may want to attend a workshop or multiple workshops on the topic. You may, on the other hand, be in the position to bring in consultants to assist you in defining the challenges in your company as well as solution pathways. To help you in making these decisions, here is a subset of companies and organizations I have found helpful, though the actual list could be a book unto itself. With descriptions from their listed websites, a starter set of these include the following:

AskNature (https://asknature.org/) – This site provides an array of nature's strategies sorted by the functions each of them accomplishes. This creates a solution bank for human design challenges consisting of almost 2,000 strategies (and probably more by the time you read this) sorted by those functions for easy use. In many cases, companies that have already applied them to useful innovations are listed as well.

The Biomimicry Institute (https://biomimicry.org/) – Their stated goal is

> for biomimicry to become a natural part of the design process. We accomplish this by tackling one massive sustainability problem at a time through our Design Challenges platform, mobilizing tens of thousands of practitioners with the support of the Global Biomimicry Network to solve the challenge, and then providing those practitioners with AskNature as a tool to begin the solution process. We anticipate dozens of new biomimetic innovations will result, creating a healthier world for all.
>
> Excerpted from the Biomimicry Institute's website 2020

The Global Biomimicry Network (https://biomimicry.org/global-networks/) – It was originally organized by the Biomimicry Institute and is made up of dozens of hubs in over 20 countries where biomimics have gathered from the Great Lakes to Great Britain, Singapore to Switzerland, and Australia to Oregon. Some are informal groups, while others work more formally on a number of company and community projects.

In addition to these programs and offerings, the Biomimicry Institute conducts a Global Design Challenge, a business launchpad for biomimicry entrepreneurs, a youth challenge, and many resources including biomimicry fellows to aid those with questions through teaching and coaching. Excerpted from the Biomimicry Institute's website 2020.

Biomimicry 3.8 (https://biomimicry.net/) – It is the leading biomimicry consultancy for businesses around the world. Operating as a certified B Corporation, B3.8 offers training and tailored consulting for businesses as well as speakers for an array of functions. Not only have they worked to help build the solution successes of Interface and Nike, they have worked with other leading companies such as GE, Seventh Generation, Kohler, Shell, and GM, as well as many other companies large and small. Excerpted from Biomimicry 3.8's website 2020.

Biomimicry Advisory Services (https://www.biomimicry-businessintelligence.com/) – It is an independent financial and market research and advisory firm, providing strategic advice and ongoing intelligence on emerging biomimicry technologies. They assist business, government, and organizations to grow a deeper understanding of biomimicry innovations and deliver facts to inform decision-making on financial investments in this emerging section. Excerpted from Biomimicry Advisory Services's website 2020.

The Biomimicry Design Alliance (https://biomimicrydesig-nalliance.org/) – It is a group of

> architects, designers, and scientists working together to create tools to make biomimicry more accessible to the architecture community. They translate the site-specific needs of the built environment into biological functions in order to solve the design challenge... BDA offers consulting services, works on unique research in architectural biomimicry, designs biomimetic projects, and educates the public on the possibilities of learning from nature as opposed to controlling it.
>
> Excerpted from the Biomimicry Design Alliance's website 2020

Biohabitats (https://www.biohabitats.com/) – It applies "the science of ecology to restoring ecosystems, conserving habitat, and regenerating the natural systems that sustain all life on Earth. We do this through engagement, assessment, planning, engineering & design, construction, and monitoring." Projects range from community or site visioning through design-build all the way to ecological restoration in from Central and North America to locations around the globe. Excerpted from Biohabitats's website 2020.

PatternFox (https://www.patternfoxconsulting.com) – PatternFox staff work with clients to apply biologically inspired design primarily to mechanical, material, and systems engineering problems. They work from ideation to design and prototyping as well as offering training. Excerpted from PatternFox's website 2020.

Symbiosis (https://www.symbiosisgroup.com/) – It is a research-driven consultancy specializing in innovation and creativity for sustainability. They combine innovation management, design thinking, and nature-based decision-making to help clients develop systemic solutions. Using ecological principles and globally place-based perspectives as a guide, they have helped clients to reconfigure supply chains, enhance operational processes, and plan for resilience in a changing business landscape. Excerpted from the Symbiosis's website 2020.

Terrapin Bright Green (https://www.terrapinbrightgreen.com/) – This design consultancy utilizes biophilia and bioinspired innovations as part of a cast of practices they bring to bear in their work. Projects range from ecological design services and technological design process mentoring to site mapping and group process charrettes for these and a host of other services impacting social, environmental, and economic goals. Excerpted from Terrapin Bright Green's website 2020.

International Living Future Institute (https://living-future.org/) – This is a nonprofit organization working in the realm of sustainability, including biophilia, primarily through their Living Building, Product, and Community Challenge programs. They also offer building energy, product ingredient, and social equity labeling programs. Excerpted from the International Living Future Institute's website 2020.

BioTRIZ (https://biotriz.com/) – BioTRIZ Ltd. Partners in TRIZ developed a "green" version of TRIZ combining successful principles and ideas used to develop solutions from nature rather than technology which they then apply to industrial problems. Bio-TRIZ consultants collaborate with domain experts on challenges to achieve practical results for companies and teach TRIZ and other creativity and innovation methods. Excerpted from the BioTRIZ's website 2020.

The Ellen MacArthur Foundation (Circular Economy) (https://www.ellenmacarthurfoundation.org/circular-economy/concept) – It is a nonprofit organization working to inspire, educate, and facilitate transition to a circular economy. The Foundation works with individuals, companies, institutions, and communities. Excerpted from the Ellen MacArthur Foundation's website 2020.

110 NOW WHAT?

Universities now offer biomimicry at the undergraduate, graduate, and postgraduate levels around the globe. Additionally, the Biomimicry Institute fellows (see www.biomimicry.org) mentioned in this book use biomimicry separately or in combination with one or more of its cousins as they work to solve problems in concert with others at their campuses and/or with companies and individuals. Most are always open to questions and new collaborations. The choice of which program or mentor best suits your needs partially depends upon which cousin you are the most interested in and what arena in which you see yourself working. Whether you are a student, a professional, or both, there are also an ever-increasing number of conferences and professional organizations addressing biomimetic questions and solution pathways.

Companies, other than those storied in this book, are also an excellent source for ideas of possible solutions in the biomimicry or biom★ workspace. By researching these and other companies using biom★, you can often learn more about the particular organism or organisms they have consulted. In some cases, they share how they went about applying nature's strategies to increase efficiencies and effectiveness along with serving people and planet in various ways and generating greater profit. Here are just some of the companies using biom★ as part of their tool bag. According to their websites and/or personal conversations with company representatives,

Aquaporin (https://aquaporin.com/) produces water filtration systems inspired by protein channels in fatty acids which allow water molecules to pass through while trapping any other particles.

Arnold Glas (https://arnold-glas.de/) created ORNILUX, a bird-friendly glass made by integrating ultraviolet (UV) technology into their panes. The technology was inspired by some types of spiders who integrate UV strands into their webs – allowing birds to avoid collisions.

Biome Renewables (https://www.biome-renewables.com/) is an industrial design firm that, among other works, developed Powercone®, a retrofitted turbine inspired by maple seeds and kingfisher beaks, which enhances both efficiency and effectiveness of wind turbines while reducing noise levels.

Blue Planet (http://www.blueplanet-ltd.com/) builds coarse-to-fine aggregates from sequestered CO_2 utilizing the carbon mineralization process and upcycled aggregates from recycled concrete.

bps (http://bps.energy/) is a clean energy company developing, among other products, BioWave. This energy-producing unit is deployed on the ocean floor and moves in a kelp-inspired manner. The resulting rocking motion allows wave energy to be transformed into energy.

Calera (http://calera.com/) harvests CO_2 from flue gases and combines it with water to form cement that reduces CO_2 output into the atmosphere while increasing the efficiency of production.

Columbia Forest Products (https://www.columbiaforest-products.com/#) uses formaldehyde-free glue in their plywood products based on the adhesion properties of the proteins found in mussels. Mussels were studied to discover how they so successfully cling to marine substrates.

Evologics (https://evologics.de/) offers solutions for subsurface communication, navigation, and monitoring based on how dolphins communicate and navigate under water.

Joinlock Pty. Ltd. (http://www.joinlox.com/) produces Joinlox™, an interlocking connection system used to build large plastic containers without the expense of having to rotomold them. Joinlox™ is constructed based on the way shellfish attach to coral and rocks and is reusable.

MOEN (https://www.moen.com/) is a plumbing fixtures company. Its designers mimicked the golden mean spiral found in the spiral of shells, the center of sunflowers, and a dizzying array of other organisms because of the efficiencies that spiral creates. By designing their flat showerhead with holes placed in that spiral, they were able to increase water-reducing efficiencies while providing full coverage for the user.

Nova Laboratories Ltd (https://www.novalabs.co.uk/) is a medical research and manufacturing company that mimicked nature's strategy to transform something from a wet state (in this case vaccines) to a dry state for storage and transport, then back back to a liquid state for use. Round worms and similar organisms provide the inspiration for this as they are able to effectively replace water in cells with a type of sugar and reanimate later as conditions allow.

Watreco (https://www.watreco.com/) is a clean tech company with an array of devices including an Industrial Vortex Generator (IVG) used to treat water and inspired by the trout's ability to remain steady in a river current.

Of course, our largest and arguably most potent resource is nature itself. All we have to do is take the steps to seek out the brilliance of nature by reading books like this; consulting biologists, designers, and engineers; and walking out into nature ourselves. By getting out there and actually observing nature – how it keeps things dry, manages energy, sheds bacteria, and covers a forest floor – we can become inspired and learn new approaches to problem-solving.

And so you have begun. You have kicked the tires. Perhaps you have found in biomimicry and biom★ a new suite of tools that will not only help you achieve a profit but help you create a better world in which you can thrive while helping others and moving toward that ultimate form of partnership found in reciprocity with the natural world. As you go about your work seeking solution pathways by consulting nature, you can also invest in reciprocity by working to save the many habitats necessary for our other earthly neighbors to live healthy robust lives. Will you take the step? The world needs you.

REFERENCES

1 Haserot, Phyllis Weiss. *You Can't Google It.* New York, NY: Morgan James Publishing. 2018.

2 "Robert Macfarlane and Barry Lopez." *YouTube.* https://www.youtube.com/watch?v=xyCFGPlLjbE. Accessed 6 February, 2020.

ONE MORE THING

How we treat our land, how we build upon it,
how we act toward our air and water,
in the long run, will tell what kind of people we really are.[1]

– Laurance S. Rockefeller

This chapter may not be for you, but it might. You've learned about biomimicry and biom* in all their forms and how a number of companies large and small have successfully used them as tools in their work. You've learned about their processes along with where they encountered bumps in the road. You've learned why they use the practices and what they have garnered in achievements to this point for doing so. You may have even already extrapolated what some of the challenges are in your workplace and where you could use one or more of these tools. You have knowledge of them and the hobgoblins you might encounter, along with a number of resources you can access to help you prepare for, plan, and deploy biomimicry or its cousins at your company.

There's just one more thing – one more opportunity I want to share while I have you here. It's something I know can benefit you and your company. It can also benefit the people beyond your company and all the living things around us. I want to talk with you about conserving habitat. If you picked up this book, you may have already had an inkling (or even full-blown knowledge) that we are supported by the global framework that is the natural world, even if you didn't think about it every day or in those exact terms. As

114 ONE MORE THING

you read, you may also have thought about local places and spaces you and your work colleagues could visit to access the strategies used by nature. With our multifaceted need for that natural framework and the brilliance held there, I think you'll agree it is illogical to continue bisecting, dissecting, or cordoning off those very ecosystems with which we are braided. We are fraying our own rope, but what can we do about it? We can embark on the journey of habitat conservation.

Before we dive in though, let me clear up the term. When we talk about "habitat conservation" for the purposes of our conversation here, I am addressing the panacea of conservation actions which assure food, water, shelter, and space in the proper arrangement for a network of living organisms. This can take the form of creating new areas of habitat appropriate to your particular location, conserving (or preserving) existing habitats, and/or restoring those damaged in some way. If you are creating new habitats or restoring existing ones, you can consult local naturalists as to what types should be located in your area, which ones may be on the decline, which would be best for your purposes, and how to go about getting started. If you are working to conserve habitats, professionals can help you there as well. All these points are within reach – just in different ways and to varying degrees.

Conserving, restoring, and creating habitat – whether on land or water – sounds like a behemoth undertaking requiring even greater business justifications than using biomimicry and biom★ by themselves. The truth is that it can be as easy as modifying the landscaping around your building or campus. On the other hand, you might want to think and act in an aspirational way to protect sections of ecosystems that need our help. In the arena of habitat conservation, you can act based on a habitat conservation Continuum of Care from the realms of economic practicality to social commitment all the way to ecological reciprocity.

We are doing "good" – whether we approach habitat conservation from a purely pragmatic economic vantage point or if we move further along the Continuum to the zone of social commitment and ecological reciprocity. Economic practicality and social commitment are both pragmatic in their own ways. But is ecological reciprocity practical as well? This depends on why we are taking action in this realm. Without judgment, we should each ask ourselves,

"Why are we embarking on this series of actions that will benefit habitat?" The answer to this question can help us make a rational plan for what we do and how we want to go about it.

Do we want to conserve, restore, or create habitat to reduce heating and cooling costs while reducing CO_2 emissions? That's economic and environmental practicality. Saving energy or water are excellent multi-service goals. We can also conserve habitat while providing other specific services like way finding, wind blocking, and pollution reduction. What a fantastic place to enter the continuum! Our company bottom line profits. Nature wins. Good for us!

We could also add another element though. As we move further down the Continuum, we can engage in social commitment where there are wins for our company and nature, but there is also some type of social service rendered. It may be that we're providing jobs to the indigenous people inhabiting a place. We may choose to provide environmental education to school or community groups to create awareness, impart knowledge, (and probably) enhance individual behaviors toward wildlife and habitats. These are also amazing places to enter the continuum! We've built a win for our company, our human, *and* our nonhuman community.

But what is ecological reciprocity and why would we travel this far down the Continuum? Reciprocity can be viewed as a kind of well-intended mutualism – returning a kindness for a kindness or a service for a service. While this may simply sound like a high form of partnership, it requires another step. The idea of ecological reciprocity is that nature has already extended a plethora of services – air to breathe, water to drink, food and materials for shelter and products, beauty, recreation, and personal restoration along with an encyclopedia of strategies from organisms and nonliving landforms and systems. Nature provides all of this to us. If we choose to participate in ecological reciprocity, we give back to nature. That's it. Nature has provided. Now we give back. What better way to give back to nature than protecting, restoring, or creating habitat?

ECONOMIC PRACTICALITY

We start from the ground up.

Any knowledgeable naturalist or landscape architect should first ask you about your intent and goals for any project small or large.

116 ONE MORE THING

But their next question or action should be to ask about or look at the soil. The "dirt" under our feet rarely gets the attention or respect it deserves. You wouldn't start a business with inferior quality materials. Likewise, if you are embarking on creating or restoring habitat around your facility, you should make sure your growing medium is fit enough to support the many organisms required to sustain whatever you plant there. Here again, we can heed Jay Harman's advice by consulting the experts. After all, you don't have to know everything! They will look at all aspects of your site: slope, moisture, amount of sun, and seasonal weather in your area affecting the site.

Once you are comfortable these things have been accounted for, you will have innumerable choices in plants. One thing in particular can make these choices easier. Choose native plants. Why? First, native plants are exactly that – native to your locale. This means they are acclimated to the soil types, general cycles of heat and cold, as well as wet and dry wherever you are located. And if you have offices in Cincinnati and Singapore, obviously you'll be using different plant species for the very different conditions in each of those places. Wherever you're located, you can consult professional resources like books and websites or take classes if you have a small business and intend to do this yourself. If your company is larger or you just don't feel like you want to take on these projects, you can also proceed directly to experienced professionals such as native plant retailers, landscape architects, government or nongovernment partners, or educators for assistance with your start-up landscaping. If you make sure they have the native plant experience you need, these pros will know what soils, specific moisture, sun, and shade requirements each plant has. This enables you, your staff, or your contractor to pick the right plant for the right place, thus reducing mortality and replanting costs. Again, whether your company is small or large, you can scale your approach.

After planting, although natives are not "no maintenance," they can be lower maintenance once fully established. Let me just repeat that last phrase, "once fully established." Any landscaping plan is going to require some amount of care early in its establishment. After that point, your cost savings become real with that lower maintenance and not having to replant as much after harsh summers or winters because you have the right plants. These cost savings multiply as we increase the square footage or acreage of our landscaped areas. In formal beds, reduced vegetation costs over time along with lower labor and maintenance costs can help you realize savings. On larger campuses, lower machinery and fuel costs also become a reality as mowed areas are transformed into native plant havens.

Once upon a time, natives were thought to look like a collection of weeds. However, as we have learned more about them, natives have sprung up in formal plantings in places as far-flung as the Sprint campus in Kansas City in the U.S.; the Xuhui Runway Park in Shanghai, China; and the Lieux publics du Projet Bonaventure streetscape in Montreal, Canada. In fact, communities around the globe have learned natives can be planted in very formal arrangements to delineate walkways, entrances, and parking zones or create striking viewsheds across large acreages. They can also separate work and play spaces or create other desired use areas.

Native plants can provide masses of color for beauty and serve as pictorial marketing tools. Unlike their exotic counterparts, many of which require planting every season, native plants can continue this cycle of multiuse by coming back every year and even reseeding themselves. With a rich color palette to choose from, these plants can create their own progression of colors from early Spring until late Fall if the right plants are selected. In the value-added realm, native plants are even being used at commercial sites for food and floriculture where businesses harvest flowers for reception desks and offer food and flowers as perks for employees and tenants.

Indeed, although these benefits are potent, natives can do double-duty by performing their various cost-saving or use-based tasks while serving as healthy sources for food, water, shelter, and space in the proper arrangement vital to an assortment of pollinators, birds, and other organisms above and below ground. Respected researcher and author Doug Tallamy underscores the differences between the effectiveness of native plants over nonnatives in a favorite comparison between a native white oak tree and a nonnative (and invasive) Bradford pear tree. In one small experiment, he compared similarly sized trees finding 410 caterpillars of almost two dozen varieties on the native oak and only 1 on the nonnative pear tree in the first round. On the second count, he found 233 caterpillars on the oak and, again, 1 on the pear tree.[2] Far from being pests, the array of insects found on the oaks feed a plethora of songbirds and other wildlife

118 ONE MORE THING

helping spur a diversity of life that stabilizes the ecology of a place – and serves to delight our eyes and ears along with those of our colleagues and clients.

In addition to transitioning beds and lawn areas to natives, companies also choose plants based on specific needs through a practice called Integrated Vegetation Management (IVM). As an example, businesses like power companies require low-growing plants under power lines to avoid entanglements. While the power companies use low-growing plants for that, taller natives can also be used to lower utility costs by creating shade in summer months or serve as windbreaks for additional energy conservation and soil protection. Other companies want physical barriers to manage noise or create pleasing line of site views. Furthermore, by blocking wind or supplying shade, such plantings are sometimes used to increase comfort levels of pedestrians moving among buildings on corporate and institutional campuses or even neighborhood development areas. Specific plants may also be used for safety as thorny natives reduce the likelihood of loitering in areas where they are planted. Still other firms, like those in the mining industry, may use IVM for remediation to a damaged area or for specific permit requirements.

One of the most common uses for native landscaping is stormwater management. Because of the absorptive property of native plant root masses, they are highly effective at both filtering pollutants and infiltrating rainfall into groundwater. These two actions provide the benefits of cleaning, slowing, and reducing the overall stormwater releases from a site. Benefits like these can be rendered by planting raingardens around downspouts, building grassy swales as catchments, and planning parking lots and campuses so rainwater drains to planted areas before leaving the site through storm drains.

In addition to providing for ground-based habitat and stormwater management, green roofs are another planting tool that can reap a number of benefits for companies while also serving nature from a higher vantage point. According to the American Society of Landscape Architects, green roofs increase insulation for buildings and provide up to a 25%[3] energy savings in the summer. From Chicago to Zurich to Singapore, designers and clients are also coming to understand vegetated rooftops can also reduce the first flush of stormwater by almost 65%. The reduction of both the amount and velocity of runoff can lead to reduced localized flooding and decreased erosion where bare soil is present. But the combination can also rejuvenate groundwater through greater infiltration in the receiving landscapes where rain gardens or other landscaping is present. In addition, because stormwater is filtered as it percolates down through the growing medium on the roof, it also results in healthier outflows.

While working with developers and landscape architects on some of the first green roofs in the Southeastern U.S., I was presented with a wonderful opportunity to see an example of this in person. As I stood in front of outfalls from adjacent buildings, downspouts carried rain from the two rooftops to the sidewalk. One building had a green roof which they used as a topyard for residents to relax, barbeque, and exercise their pets. The building next door had a standard roof. As I stood there in the pouring rain, I was gobsmacked by the difference in water transfer. The downspout from the standard roof was gushing water onto the sidewalk and out to the storm drain. The building with the green roof was transporting its water load at a dribble.

This all happens because green roofs increase a building site's overall pervious surface. Unlike impervious surfaces such as parking lots, traditional roofs, and sidewalks, pervious rain gardens, swales, and green roofs allow for those greater levels of filtration and infiltration. Recognizing this, a number of cities in the U.S. from San Francisco and Portland to Boston and Washington, D.C., are either requiring green roofs or offering incentives of different types for developers who install them. In Europe, countries such as France, Denmark, and Switzerland have acted in a similar fashion along with cities such as Tokyo and Toronto, making green roofs a tool worldwide.

A further cost saving of green roofs is the fact they can extend roof life by two to three times because of the damage resulting from surface overheating on standard roofs. If we summarize all those savings, even though green roofs are more expensive at the outset, we can see many opportunities for substantial positive impacts in operating, marketing, and even capital budgets while creating usable space for wildlife along with areas for meetings or lunch spots for employees. Decision-makers from large corporations such as Ford Motor Company and small ones such as South Africa's Homini Hotel along with designers of landmarks such as China's Nanyang

120 ONE MORE THING

School of Art and New York City's Jacob K. Javits Convention Center have installed green roofs both small and large to great effect. In addition, managers of park buildings, office complexes, and even presidential libraries have recognized benefits of greening their topsides.

But wait, there's more. If you choose to use native plants, you also create a productive research and development lab for biomimicry and biom★. Team members can visit native landscaping areas to learn how to retain or deflect fluids as they observe a variety of plants. They can learn more about locomotion, transportation, and distribution as they watch birds, bees, ants, and even flowering plants as they disperse seed. They can learn about biom★ used in packaging as they examine shells of nuts, containers surrounding galls, and the protective structures of pinecones. They can even learn how nature creates color through structure by investigating butterflies. What's more, since they are native plants aligned with the conditions in your location, you can be sure solutions inspired by or mimicking the strategies you observe are likely to work where your business is located. All of these practices reflect the "economically practical" end of the habitat conservation Continuum of Care.

SOCIAL RECIPROCITY

As we move toward the center of the Continuum, we can add to our economic benefits by participating in or creating social reciprocity. In the social realm, reciprocity entails reaching out to people within and beyond the company to educate, lift up, and activate them in service of nature. The benefits of action here go to the people and the environment as well as the business itself. Companies such as CRH Americas Materials, DTE Energy, and General Motors are conserving, creating, and/or restoring habitats by engaging employees, students, and community members in those projects. These corporate citizens are supplying a place where people can learn about plant species attributes, requirements, and the importance of protecting them along with the pollinators, birds, mammals, and many other species dependent upon them. While there, people can also learn about crucial local habitats – the forests, rivers, lakes, prairies, and other wild spaces these plants, animals, and other organisms call home.

Many times, companies will partner with community members along with local nonprofit or educational groups or international organizations such as the Wildlife Habitat Council and Conservation International, among a legion of others. As they do this, they can begin to offset negative industrial impacts with positive outreach and commitment to habitat. This turns a swath of human potential energy into positive actions.

They do this in neighborhoods, in parks and public conservation areas, at schools, and even in specific on-site company conservation areas. They work on habitat creation and protection but also support work of this type by printing educational materials, sponsoring events, and supporting programs that magnify their reach from company to organizations and the public. The practical side of these actions includes good marketing and good will. But these conservation and education programs can move a company further down the Continuum to a place of raising participant and company awareness to shape positive intent and change the behaviors of all participants toward and with the environment. Companies such as Bridgestone Americas sponsor events that reach multigenerational audiences to raise awareness and increase knowledge about nature. In Quebec, Bridgestone Canada supported a conservation organization by funding bilingual butterfly publications for events focused on wildlife around the L'Assomption River. In the U.S., Bridgestone Americas supported watershed health by sponsoring community stakeholder meetings and ongoing dragonboat races on the Cumberland River. This drew people out on a waterway they formerly thought of as too polluted for play. Further south in Monterrey, the local Bridgestone México plant worked with a local organization to fund, develop, and distribute a family-oriented bird guidebook to schools and tourism sites. Such actions can entertain and educate while leading nearby residents to protect and promote biodiversity in the areas where these activities are taking place.

Another form of habitat protection, restoration, and creation can be seen with Daikin Industries' "Forests for the Air" project. Around the globe in China, Japan, India, Cambodia, Indonesia, Liberia, and Brazil, Daikin is partnering with an international nonprofit, local governments, employees, and local residents to train local residents as rangers and land managers. In other areas, they are teaching and supporting locals by offering new nature-friendly farming practices

122 ONE MORE THING

which provide income while protecting the habitats from former abuses. These acts of habitat conservation through education and employment creation for local people have had a beneficial impact for both the forests and the people who live there. It is not yet ecological reciprocity, but it is moving in that direction.

ECOLOGICAL RECIPROCITY

Back in Chapter 1, you read about a model of global citizenry which encompasses all living things including us. This place, this planet contains our community. We are actually planetary citizens in a planetary community. Microsoft's Siri includes, as its very last definition of community, "a group of interdependent organisms of different species growing or living together in a specified habitat." Whether we're urbanites in a desert area, suburbanites in the mountains, exurbanites on the plains, or people in rural areas by the sea, we are all in some type of relationship with whatever forms of nature surround us. We are interdependent beings relying on the frameworks of multilayered habitats providing for food, water, shelter, and space in the proper arrangement. Increasingly, we are also beginning to understand that the beauty of wild places and even gardens outside our offices also contributes to our sense of well-being.

Florence Williams, in her book *The Nature Fix: Why Nature Makes us Happier, Healthier, and More Creative*, noted from her research,

> We don't experience natural environments enough to realize how restored they can make us feel, nor are we aware that studies also show they make us healthier, more creative, more empathetic and more apt to engage with the world and with each other. Nature, it turns out, is good for civilization.[4]

So our neighbors should all count – whether they are the lilies of Kazakhstan, the Pallid harriers of Algeria, Sun bears from Thailand, Oregon morels, whales off the coast of Mexico, your mail carrier, and great aunt Edith. Together we are a planetary community.

Within that community we all have different roles. We sometimes break these down into subgroups such as predator and prey, decomposers, producers, consumers, animals, plants, and fungi. Ray Anderson

ONE MORE THING **123**

was intrigued by Daniel Quinn's assignments of "givers" and "takers"[5] as roles in our communities. After reading Ray's book and subsequently Mr. Quinn's, of course I was determined to be a giver.

But as I've thought more deeply about these books, roles and reciprocity itself, I think I see where I may have gone a little wrong. When we hear the words "taker," "consumer," or "predator," a very distinct feeling comes to mind. As a biologist, the second two don't give me pause because they are just part of my work. However, long ago before I was a biologist or a teacher, I was just a little tyke watching Mutual of Omaha's Wild Kingdom on Sunday night television. There, I must confess, consumer and predator didn't figure into my sense of parity. I rarely rooted for the lion or the shark.

"Run little antelope! Swim little seal!"

In general, terms such as "predator" and "taker" can be loaded with negative connotations in any language. We are taught from a young age that taking is bad and giving is good. Because of these teachings in early life, the words and the actions connected with them have taken on values of good and bad, acceptable and unacceptable.

How confusing then to enter the world of business where we are taught as adults to "grab" market shares and "maximize" profits. Then we are rewarded for achieving those things. Cost minimization, asset stripping, and takeovers seem to be the opposite of what we were taught as children. So we're left in a weird limbo as to what we should strive for and hold in the highest esteem. Is it a case of making a living first and worrying about contributing to others after all business goals have been achieved? Has the term "ecological reciprocity" occurred in a single business text?

And yet, it does occur – at least the beginnings of it.

Ecological reciprocity is the concept and attendant action of giving back to a habitat or its larger ecosystem because it has already given much to us. If it is real reciprocity, it is given with no strings attached. We have received multitudes from nonliving elements such as water, wind, and sun along with accepting much from other living organisms. It stands to reason we should give back to create the state of mutual benefit.

Having said that, we know Earth doesn't exist in a static state. Those cycles within cycles continue to operate. Trees keep pumping out oxygen while taking in CO_2. Wild blackberries and persimmons

124 ONE MORE THING

find their way to dinner tables as their seeds are distributed by birds to grow elsewhere. Bamboo still holds up our roofs, covers our floors, provides eating utensils, and even socks as its rhizomes continue to spread and grow. What is our place in these cycles? Because nature continues to give, it seems logical that we should accept that while persistently looking for ways we can give back to nature – not *in exchange for* these materials and services but *because* of them. The more we provide without thought of returns, the further down the Continuum we travel.

The Walt Disney Company has moved from social reciprocity into the early stages of ecological reciprocity through their Disney Climate Solutions Fund,[6] which has funded forest conservation projects in the U.S., China, Mexico, and Peru from company coffers. They didn't begin with ecological reciprocity however. They began their environmental work in the economically practical areas of fuel conservation and use of alternative fuels. After they tended to these areas, they began working with Conservation International to create educational programs with coffee farmers in Peru. By bringing in techniques to cultivate shade-grown coffee and collaborating to create conservation agreements with farmers, the partners were able to have a positive impact on climate change and enhance biodiversity on over 450,000 acres of the Alto Mayo in Peru. In the process, they have garnered a new environmentally friendly source of coffee for Disney properties and visitors. But the larger point connected to ecological reciprocity is the continued protection and restoration of the Alto Mayo.

Turning again to Bridgestone Americas as an example, we see another company with projects all along the Continuum. It's important to remember that this Continuum of Care hosts some type of restoration, conservation/preservation, and/or creation at all points along its line. In Bridgestone's case, they have created habitat surrounding many of their facilities where plants and animals can survive unmolested and mowed areas have been sliced to a minimum. In this, we see an example of economic practicality as mowers remain at the edges of roadways and sidewalks, use less fuel and manpower, and depreciate at a reduced rate while habitat is protected. The sites are also used for social reciprocity because they play a critical role as settings for local science curriculums with over 25,000 students served to date. And when they donated 10,000 acres of land as a wildlife management area to the state of Tennessee in the U.S., they traveled into the beginnings of ecological reciprocity.

Greer Tidwell, Director of Environmental Management at Bridgestone, had this to say,

> We created a value structure that created the continuum from saving resources like fuel, to supporting environmental education to saving wild spaces. We manage our own habitat sites thoughtfully and humbly.

So far, Bridgestone Americas has donated almost 16,000 acres for habitat in total. Donations of land like this are a form of reciprocity because although they may carry the company name and perhaps some tax benefits over a few years, the donors have created a situation where other living things receive protection of their habitat permanently. In addition to conservation agreements and outright donations, companies can also use the tool of creating conservation easements to support habitat on specified parcels of land. Conservation easements are very individualized and can allow for some uses while prohibiting others depending on the owner's intent and goals. Land trusts are primary partners to create conservation easements and can walk company personnel through the steps to accomplish them. Additional organizations like those mentioned and others who might be local to your site are available for consultation and partnerships to achieve conservation agreements and land donations.

It is notable that even with all this good work along the Continuum, there are still few, if any, companies that have ventured fully into the heart of ecological reciprocity. Because they are businesses, there always seem to be some attachments to economic practicality or social reciprocity. This isn't what I'd call bad. It's what I'd call a good start. Those companies that have protected land in even small ways deserve some credit – and for those that have gone further, even more credit.

Biomimicry and its cousins are methods we can use in our companies to build better sportswear, carpeting, heating and cooling units, fans, bacteria-shedding materials, and a host of other products and processes. Inspired by organisms in the natural world around us, we are creating new tools to save energy and materials, reduce waste, and even heal. Learning from nature can bring you into this space. Communicating your intent and measuring your results can keep you there. But understanding and supporting the actions that allow our nonhuman neighbors the ability to live and thrive in their natural habitat is worth at least as much as better projects and good public relations. It's what makes us good neighbors in our communities.

ACKNOWLEDGMENTS

A portion of this chapter is based on an interview conducted in March 2020 with Greer Tidwell. I thank Greer for sharing his time, descriptions of Bridgestone Americas, and their conservation journey. *−MF*

REFERENCES

1 *United States, Beauty for America Proceedings of the White House Conference on Natural Beauty.* Government Printing Office, 1965.

2 Tallamy, Douglas W. "The Chickadee's Guide to Gardening". *The New York Times.* March 11, 2015.

3 American Society of Landscape Architects. "Increasing Energy Efficiency: Residential Green Roofs." https://www.asla.org/residentialgreenroofs.aspx. Accessed 6 February, 2020.

4 Williams, Florence. *The Nature Fix: Why Nature Makes us Happier, Healthier, and More Creative.* New York, NY: W. W. Norton Company. 2017.

5 Quinn, D. *Ishmael an Adventure of the Mind and Spirit.* New York, NY: Bantam Books, 1992.

6 The Walt Disney Company. https://thewaltdisneycompany.com/disney-brings-conservation-efforts-peru-u-s-parks-resorts/. Accessed 3 March, 2020.

AFTERWORD

What do we do when we network with each other? We greet one another in a style we deem acceptable in the culture and surroundings we inhabit at the time. We ask each other questions to express interest and learn more about the being with whom we are talking. We learn from them, and if they give us information we can use, we adopt it and thank them for it. We have the opportunity to do the same with nature through biomimicry and biom★.

I have many to thank in the completion of this book. First, both formally and informally, I must thank nature itself. I try to do this every day by acknowledging an individual – a maple tree, a chickadee, a porcelain-colored mushroom in a fairy ring. Their ways of interacting with the world have bestowed upon me beauty and peace, motivation, and wonderful information to guide my life whether the lesson has been about cycles of rest, industry, communication or those of living in general. Janine Benyus expanded my view to see how we could interact with nature if we chose (and certainly need to) as business and community citizens. Organisms can be our inspiration and instructors for problem-solving in business as well as in our cities and towns. Certainly they are neighbors deserving the care and respect reciprocity bestows. Janine has also been a whip-smart teacher and caring colleague. I give her leagues of love and thanks. My other human teachers – Karen Allen, Sherry Ritter, Chris Montero, Juan Rovalo, and Dayna Baumeister – made manifest the world of biomimicry and its methods for which I am grateful.

In learning, one can hopefully experience the bounty of energy and innovative thought colleagues can bring. I was blessed with all

128 AFTERWORD

that and friendship too in Moana Lebel, Karen Frasier-Scott, Marie Zanowick, Megan Schuknecht, Heidi Fischer, Marjan Eggermont, Norbert Hoeller, Richard MacCowan, Cindy Spiva-Evans, Curt McNamara, Taryn Mead, Ashok Goel, Mariappan "Jawa" Jawaharlal, Raúl de Villafranca, Karen Rossin Johnson, Beth Brummitt, Sandra Dudley, Alëna Louguina, Bas Sanders, and Bob Willard.

Of special note in the writing of this book are two people. Ray Anderson ran a company that embodied the phrase "doing well by doing good." He lived it. He was it. His was the first corporate sustainability report I ever saw, and it drove me to further engage with businesses. Second, Jacques Chirazi's application of business knowledge in the field of biomimicry and this book in particular have been crucial and his friendship – unable to be mimicked.

At the very beginnings of the writing, I just wanted to answer the questions my Lipscomb University sustainability MBA students were asking. Thank heavens and thanks to program director Dodd Galbreath who saw fit to send me packing to Costa Rica to learn. H. Emerson (Chip) Blake and author Robert Michael (Bob) Pyle gave me the writing tools and encouragement to better translate nature to the page at Orion's Wildbranch Writing Workshop for which I am tremendously appreciative. Out of that came the Wildlings who wear each other's work as it's being tailored, extoling, and adjusting as needed. Our monthly sharing has allowed this second family of especially Gavin Van Horn and Sara Crosby along with Missy Wick, David Taylor, and Sara Beck to serve as my piers of support and my touchstones. You are all gossamer and oak.

A book of stories, whether to reveal or simply entertain, would be nothing without the cast of characters who were the guideposts for this volume. I wanted to thank each interviewee from the companies whose stories I have told in this book at the culmination of their chapters. Without each of them, there would be no book at all.

But the stories would never work without good editors. Thank you to Susan Marsh and Florence Williams for reviewing and artfully suggesting places to nip and expand. Thanks also to Rebecca Marsh and Sophie Peoples and all the kind and knowledgeable professionals at Routledge, without whom I would still be staring at manuscript pages instead of a full-blown book. Kindness and patience do still exist in the world and they are the evidence.

Portions of "Business from the Wild – Interface, Inc." first appeared in *Wildness: Relations of People and Place*, the University of Chicago Press, Chicago and London. Thank you to Christy Henry, Gavin again, and John Hausdoerffer for seeing promise in the wilds and my work.

Friendship fuels the ship once launched, and I would be lost without Gail and Jim Current, Barb and Dennis Radford-Kapp, Vera and Wesley Roberts, Rena and Jim Wray-Davis, Marc Alston, Patty Cantrell, and Justine Lines who are always ready to fill my sails.

Finally, I would be a lonely cedar without my Jim, Carly, and Zach. Your reading, listening, encouragement, and love powered me through this and all things.

#

INDEX

Acacia tree 86
Adelphia Communications 67
Alto Mayo 124
American Chemical Society 90
American Society of Landscape
  Architects 118
Anderson, Ray 37–41, 45, 70, 86,
  102–103, 122–123
ants 20, 74, 76, 78, 80, 83, 86, 120
Aquaporin 110
Aristotle 25, 87
Arnold Glas 110
AskNature 107

bacteria 26, 28, 65–72, 87
Bagan, Joe 67, 72
bats 27
Baumeister, Dayna 15, 17, 24, 32,
  39, 41, 47, 92–93
bees 74–85, 95, 120
Bell, Alexander Graham 71
Benyus, Janine 6–7, 15–16, 24, 28,
  41, 92–93; *Biomimicry: Innovation
  Inspired by Nature* 7
Berra, Yogi 21
biochemical communication 76–77
Biohabitats 108
bio-inspiration 27, 58; and Nike 20, 23
Biologists at the Design Table 17
biom* 28, 60, 91–95, 100, 102–106,
  110, 112–114, 120
Biome Renewables 110

biomimetics 27–28
biomimicry 74, 76, 79; books on
  105–106; and business 7–9, 36; as
  business practice 84; defined 12;
  and diversity 41; Encycle 81–82,
  84; Interface 87, 93; and life
  cycles 39–40; and natural world
  100; Nike and 93; at Oakey
  Design 47; overview 23–34; at
  PAX 58 reasons for companies
  using 91–92, 125–126; and
  reciprocity 92–93; rules of 29–31;
  success of 95; and sustainability 17;
  as a tool for enhanced business
  outcomes 86; as a tool for human
  benefits 86; as a tool for language
  98; as a tool for sustainability 86
Biomimicry 3.8 107–108; *see also*
  Biomimicry Guild
Biomimicry Advisory Group 8
Biomimicry Advisory Services 108
The Biomimicry Design Alliance 108
Biomimicry Guild 16, 24
*Biomimicry: Innovation Inspired by
  Nature* (Janine) 7
Biomimicry Institute 28, 31, 107, 110
bionics 26, 104
biophilia 12, 24, 58, 104, 109;
  applications of 25; design 25
BioTRIZ 26–27, 104, 109
bio-utilization 25–26
blackout 75

132 INDEX

Blue Planet 93, 110
BMW 81
boat designing 53–56
bottom line 87
boundaries 30, 33, 40, 91–92, 96, 100
bps 111
BPS bioWAVE 95
Bradford, John 39, 42–45
Brennan, Anthony 62, 72, 102
Bridgestone Americas, Inc. 70, 121, 124–125
Bridgestone Canada 121
Bridgestone México 121
bull kelp 95
business: and biomimicry 7–9, 36; innovation and nature 58–59; and partnerships 2–5, 82–83; and raw materials 2–3; *see also* business models
business models: emulating nature 4–5; and nature 3–4; at Nike 13

cactus 33
Calera 111
calla lilies 56
Callow, James 63
Callow, Maureen 63
cataracts 70
CCI 81
Centers for Disease Control and Prevention 67
Chemistry Innovation Knowledge Transfer Network 90
chrematistics 87
Chirazi, Jacques 8
citizen-driven model 6–7
citizenship 6, 13, 19–20
Climate Neutral Network 48
closed-loop system 16, 44, 91
Cohen, Ben 86
Columbia Forest Products 111
Columbia Wood Products 95
company inertia, overcoming 102–112
conservation easements 125

Conservation International 121, 124
consumer-driven model 6
Continuum of Care 114–115, 120–121, 124–125
Cook Medical 69, 71
Cool Carpet™ 48
Coors Biomedical 64, 66
corporate sustainability 1, 48
corporate sustainability reports 1, 82
creating: intentions 98–102; new language 98–102
CRH Americas Materials 120
Crosbie, Dick 13
cycles 3, 18–19, 40, 123; life cycle 39; nature 30, 33, 37–38; water 30
cyclic processes 30, 40

Daikin Industries: "Forests for the Air" project 121; habitat protection, restoration, and creation 121–122
Daniel, Sydney 41, 46, 47
Department of Defense (DOD) 68
Department of Fisheries and Wildlife 52
Design Table (BaDT) 17
Discovery Channel 66
Disney Climate Solutions Fund 124
disruptive technologies 71
diversity: and biomimicry 41; Sydney Daniel on 47
Donne, John 36
DTE Energy 120
dynamic nonequilibrium 31, 40

ecological reciprocity 114–115, 122–126
economic practicality 114, 115–120, 125
Ecovative Design 26
Edison, Thomas 74
The Ellen MacArthur Foundation 109
emulating nature, 7, 9, 20, 24, 43
Emergence (Johnson) 74
emergent systems 74, 76, 82

INDEX **133**

Encycle 34, 74–85, 81, 92–93; lessons learned 82–84
energy: BioWave and 95, 111; conservation of 66, 118; Encycle, use of 81–83, 87; green roofs and 118; Japan Railway West and requirement of 5; Lotusan® and requirement of 6; nature and 33, 80; renewable 49; use in the U.S. 58, 75–77; World Economic Forum's Global Risks Report 2020 on 90
entrepreneur 29, 58, 93, 102, 106
Entropy™ 41, 46–47
Escherichia coli (*E. coli*) 65–67
Evologics 111

fear of being wrong 103
FedEx 48
feedback loops 77
FLEXcon 71
Florida Institute of Technology 64
Foley catheter 68
Ford Motor Company 119
forest product industry 2
Friton, Mike 12
frogs 17
Fromm, Erich 25
functional challenges 91–92, 105
fungi 86–87, 95

Garvis, Greg 66–67
Gatorade 66
GE 108
General Motors 108, 120
genius of place 36–37
geckos 14, 16
Genomatica 48
The Global Biomimicry Network 107
global citizen-driven model 7, 19, 88
Goat Tek 12, 13, 20
Gray, Elisha 71
green roofs 118–120

green rubber 16, 18, 20, 24
greenwashing 88–89, 104

habitat conservation 114, 120, 122
Harman, Jay 51–61, 102–103, 116; boat designing 53–56; on movement within nature 52–53
Haserot, Phyllis Weiss 97
Hawken, Paul 38
heating, ventilation, and air conditioning (HVAC) systems 78, 80, 84
Heraclitus 31, 33
Herr, Hugh 26
hobgoblins: of greenwashing 104; overcoming 102–112
Holling, C. S. 40
Homini Hotel 119
hospital-acquired infections 70
hospitals: infections in 67–68, 70, 87; nurse sharks in 62–72

i2® 48
Industrial Revolution 37–38, 98
inertia (overcoming) 102
Integrated Vegetation Management (IVM) 118
intentions, creating 97–102
Interface, Inc. 34, 37–49, 92–93, 95, 107; and human intentions 43–44; lessons learned by 46–49; optimization, language of 45; sustainability at 39; sustainability vision of 37, 39; waste reduction 43
internal biological programming 77
International Living Future Institute 109

Jacob J. Javits Convention Center 120
Japan Railway West 5
Johnson, Steven: *Emergence* 74
Joinlock Pty. Ltd. 111
Jones, Bill 39, 41–42

Kerbel, Mark 74–85
kingfishers 4–5
Kohler 108
Kulyk, Roman 74–81

134 INDEX

land trusts 125
language: biomimicry as 98–102; creating new 98–102
LG International 69
Life Cycle Assessment 39
life cycles and biomimicry 39–40
life-friendly practices/chemistry 13–14, 16, 20, 32, 34, 37
Life's Principles 32, 49, 66
lily impeller 57, 59–60, 87, 95
limits 30, 33, 40, 65
Lopez, Barry 97–99
lotus plants 4
Lotusan 4, 6
Louisville Slugger 3

McDonough, Bill 17, 21
Macfarlane, Robert 97
market penetration 60
market saturation 71
Maslow, Abraham 89
Massachusetts Institute of Technology (MIT) 26
meeting people where they are 103
Mercurial Superfly 360 19
Mestral, George de 23
Methicillin-resistant Staphylococcus aureus (MRSA) 68
Michaels 81
MOEN 111
mountain goats 11–13, 19, 27, 95
Museum of Natural History (Florida) 64
mussels 14

Nanyang School of Art 120
National Aeronautics and Space Administration 90
National Institutes of Health (NIH) 68–69
National Oceanic and Atmospheric Administration 90
native plants 46, 116–118, 120
natural pattern, 12
natural resources 2–3, 5–6, 13–14, 30, 69–70, 88, 91

nature: and adaptations 32–33; adapting strategies from, in business 5; and business innovation 58–59; conservation for economic benefits 5; and creativity 59; cycles 30, 37–38; genius of place 36–37; mimicking 36–37, 52, 59; movement within 52–53; optimization, language of 45; patterns and principles 48; professional training 1; and use of cycles 33
The Nature Fix: Why Nature Makes us Happier, Healthier, and More Creative (Williams) 12, 122
nature's genius 6–7, 16–17, 46, 58
nature's operating conditions 29–32, 40, 46
nature's spirals 56
new language, creating 98–102
niche market 34
Nike 21, 24, 48, 87, 92–93, 107; BaDT 17; and bio-inspiration 20; global citizen-driven model 19; Lessons Learned 19–22; mountain goat feet features in shoes 11–12; sustainable business strategies 15; water-based adhesives 14
Nike Air 16
nitrogen 30
Nova Laboratories Ltd 111

Oakey, David 37–39, 41–42, 46, 48
Oakey Design 37; biomimicry at 47; and sustainability 38; sustainability vision of 37–38; waste reduction 43
octopus 17, 27
Office of Naval Research 62
Oikonomia 87, 95
operating conditions 29–32, 40, 46
optimization 21, 45, 59, 66
ORNILUX (bird-friendly glass) 94, 110
Outboard Marine Corporation (OMC) 55
owls 4–5

INDEX **135**

partnerships 82–83, 96; and business 2–5; human, with living organisms 4
PatternFox 108
patterns 43, 47, 48–49, 77, 83, 87; deep 24, 27, 29, 32; natural 12; pay attention to 31–32
PAX 34, 87, 92–93, 95; Lessons Learned 58–61
PAX Air 58
PAX Mixer 57–58
PAX Pure 58
PAX Scientific 56–61
PAX Water Technologies 58, 60
Peaceful Union 72
peak demand 78, 84
Pearl Harbor 62–63
Petco 81
Pier 1 81
Pond Studio 46
professional training, and nature 1
profit: and biomimicry 34, 90, 92–93, 95, 99, 110, 112, 115, 123; business 37, 40, 45–46, 49; and Encycle 87; and environmental sustainability 87–88, 91, 95; global citizenship 20; and Nike 13, 21, 24, 87; and PAX 56; research and development 60; and Sharklet 71

Quinn, Daniel 38, 123

raw materials, and nature 2–3, 29, 44–45
reciprocity 2–3, 5–6, 8–9, 29, 33–34, 44, 69–70, 86–90, 93, 95, 98, 101, 104–106, 112 community-building 90; ecological 114–115, 120, 122–125; social 120–122, 124–125
REGEN: electrical transmitter of 78; established in 76; HVAC compact sensors 79–81
regenerative practices 84, 104, 106
research and development (R&D) 60, 120
resilience 13, 75, 91, 95, 109
rolling around 31

Sage Hill School 81
Sappi North America 69, 71
Schmitt, Otto 12, 24
Sears 81
Seff, Dan 67
self-actualization 89
self-organizing system 77
Seventh Generation 108
shark 64–66, 95, 123
Sharklet Technologies, Inc. 34, 62–72, 92–93, 95; Cook Medical, collaboration with 71; lessons learned 69–72; patents and 71
Shell 108
Shinkansen train 4, 8, 102
Small Business Innovation Research program 68
social commitment 114
social insects 77
social reciprocity 120–122, 124–125
Speicker, Mark 67, 72
spiders 27
Sports Authority 81
Staphylococcus aureus (Staph) 67, 68
starfish 17
Steelcase 69
stewardship 81, 87–91
StoColor 4
Sto Corporation 4, 8
sun power 30
sustainability 86–87, 91–92, 95, 106–107, 109; and biomimicry 17; in business 8, 37; corporate 1, 48; Encycle 75, 82, 84; framework for Nike 15–17, 19, 22; at Interface 37–40, 45 Oakey Design 37–38
sustainable business strategies 15
Swain, Geoff 64
swarm based algorithms 76, 78–79
Symbiosis 109

Tallamy, Doug 117
target market 67, 84
Terrapin Bright Green 109
Theory of Inventive Problem Solving (TRIZ) 26

136 INDEX

Tidwell, Greer 125, 126
Third-party verification 83
triple bottom line 8, 69, 88–89

Ultracane 27
Ulva linza zoospores 63
University of Birmingham 63
University of Florida 62, 72

Velcro 23
Veterans Administration 68
Vinci, Leonardo da 23
volatile organic compounds (VOCs)
    13–14

Walt Disney Company 124
water-based adhesives 13–14
water cycle 30
Watreco 111
Wildlife Habitat Protection
    Council 121
Wild Thing craft 53, 56
Williams, Florence 12, 122
Wilson, E. O. 25
Winslow, Darcy 13–15, 17–19,
    21, 22, 29
World Economic Forum's
    Global Risks Report
    2020 90